50 Washington State Recipes for Home

By: Kelly Johnson

Table of Contents

- Salmon with Maple Glaze
- Dungeness Crab Cakes
- Pacific Northwest Clam Chowder
- Cedar-Plank Grilled Salmon
- Washington Apple Crisp
- Marionberry Pie
- Wild Mushroom Risotto
- Smoked Steelhead Trout
- Apple Cider Braised Pork
- Columbia River Salmon Steaks
- Seattle-Style Hot Dogs
- Washington Berry Cobbler
- Roasted Garlic and Herb Chicken
- Northwest Seafood Stew
- Huckleberry Pancakes
- Baked Alaskan Salmon with Dill
- Sweet Corn and Crab Chowder
- Blackberry and Apple Sauce
- Grilled Wild Salmon Tacos
- Washington State BBQ Ribs
- Clam Linguine
- Honey-Glazed Roasted Carrots
- Berry-Lemon Muffins
- Pacific Northwest Meatloaf
- Mushroom and Swiss Quiche
- Huckleberry Jam
- Roasted Beet Salad with Goat Cheese
- Salmon and Asparagus Foil Packets
- Cherry-Limeade
- Washington State-style Pot Roast
- Apple and Sausage Stuffing
- Lemon and Herb Grilled Chicken
- Wild Mushroom and Barley Soup
- Roasted Brussels Sprouts with Bacon
- Northwest Berry Smoothie
- Washington Apple Salad

- Salmon and Potato Chowder
- Blackberry Crumble Bars
- Pan-Seared Dungeness Crab
- Herb-Crusted Roasted Chicken
- Pacific Northwest Pumpkin Soup
- Apple-Walnut Pancakes
- Spicy Salmon Sushi Rolls
- Clam and Corn Bake
- Cherry-Almond Coffee Cake
- Grilled Portobello Mushrooms
- Washington State Fruit Tart
- Spaghetti with Tomato and Basil
- Crab-Stuffed Mushrooms
- Marionberry and Cream Cheese Bars

Salmon with Maple Glaze

Ingredients:

- 4 salmon fillets
- 1/4 cup pure maple syrup
- 2 tablespoons soy sauce
- 1 tablespoon Dijon mustard
- 1 tablespoon olive oil
- 2 cloves garlic, minced
- 1 teaspoon fresh lemon juice
- 1/2 teaspoon ground black pepper
- 1/2 teaspoon salt
- Optional: chopped fresh parsley for garnish

Instructions:

1. **Preheat Oven:**
   - Preheat your oven to 400°F (200°C).
2. **Prepare the Glaze:**
   - In a small bowl, whisk together the maple syrup, soy sauce, Dijon mustard, olive oil, minced garlic, lemon juice, black pepper, and salt.
3. **Prepare the Salmon:**
   - Place the salmon fillets on a baking sheet lined with parchment paper or aluminum foil.
4. **Glaze the Salmon:**
   - Brush the salmon fillets generously with the maple glaze mixture.
5. **Bake:**
   - Bake in the preheated oven for about 12-15 minutes, or until the salmon is cooked through and flakes easily with a fork. The cooking time may vary depending on the thickness of the fillets.
6. **Serve:**
   - Remove the salmon from the oven and brush with additional glaze if desired. Garnish with chopped fresh parsley if using.
7. **Enjoy:**
   - Serve the glazed salmon with your favorite side dishes, such as roasted vegetables, rice, or a fresh salad.

This dish is sweet, savory, and has a lovely balance of flavors. Enjoy!

Dungeness Crab Cakes

Ingredients:

- **Crab Cakes:**
    - 1 lb Dungeness crab meat, picked over for shells
    - 1/2 cup mayonnaise
    - 1 large egg
    - 1 tablespoon Dijon mustard
    - 1 tablespoon lemon juice
    - 1 teaspoon Old Bay seasoning (or more to taste)
    - 1/4 cup finely chopped fresh parsley
    - 1/4 cup finely chopped green onions
    - 1/2 cup panko breadcrumbs (plus more for coating)
    - 2 tablespoons olive oil (for frying)
- **Remoulade Sauce (optional):**
    - 1/2 cup mayonnaise
    - 1 tablespoon Dijon mustard
    - 1 tablespoon lemon juice
    - 1 tablespoon chopped fresh parsley
    - 1 teaspoon hot sauce (adjust to taste)
    - Salt and pepper to taste

Instructions:

1. **Prepare the Crab Meat:**
    - Gently pick through the crab meat to ensure there are no shell fragments.
2. **Mix the Crab Cake Mixture:**
    - In a large bowl, combine the mayonnaise, egg, Dijon mustard, lemon juice, Old Bay seasoning, parsley, green onions, and 1/2 cup of panko breadcrumbs. Mix well.
3. **Fold in the Crab Meat:**
    - Gently fold in the crab meat, being careful not to break up the lumps too much. The mixture should hold together but still be light and fluffy.
4. **Form the Crab Cakes:**
    - Shape the mixture into 8-10 patties, depending on the size you prefer. Dredge each patty lightly in additional panko breadcrumbs, pressing gently to adhere.
5. **Cook the Crab Cakes:**
    - Heat olive oil in a large skillet over medium heat. Once the oil is hot, add the crab cakes. Cook for about 3-4 minutes on each side, or until golden brown and crispy. Be careful when flipping them to avoid breaking.
6. **Make the Remoulade Sauce (if using):**
    - In a small bowl, combine all the remoulade sauce ingredients and mix well. Adjust seasoning to taste.
7. **Serve:**

        - Serve the crab cakes warm, with a dollop of remoulade sauce on the side or drizzled over the top.
8. **Enjoy:**
        - These crab cakes are great with a simple salad, coleslaw, or as part of a seafood feast.

Enjoy your Dungeness crab cakes!

Pacific Northwest Clam Chowder

Ingredients:

- **For the Chowder:**
    - 4 strips bacon, chopped
    - 1 medium onion, finely chopped
    - 2 cloves garlic, minced
    - 2 celery stalks, diced
    - 2 medium potatoes, peeled and diced
    - 1 cup carrots, diced
    - 1/2 cup dry white wine (optional)
    - 4 cups chicken or vegetable broth
    - 2 cups heavy cream
    - 2 cups canned clams, drained (reserve the juice)
    - 1 cup reserved clam juice
    - 1 tablespoon chopped fresh thyme
    - 1 tablespoon chopped fresh parsley
    - 1 bay leaf
    - Salt and pepper to taste
    - 2 tablespoons all-purpose flour (optional, for thickening)
- **For Garnish (optional):**
    - Fresh chopped parsley
    - Lemon wedges
    - Oyster crackers or crusty bread

Instructions:

1. **Cook the Bacon:**
    - In a large pot or Dutch oven, cook the chopped bacon over medium heat until crispy. Remove the bacon bits with a slotted spoon and set aside, leaving the rendered fat in the pot.
2. **Sauté Vegetables:**
    - Add the chopped onion to the pot with the bacon fat and cook until translucent, about 3-4 minutes.
    - Add the minced garlic, celery, carrots, and potatoes. Cook for another 5 minutes, stirring occasionally.
3. **Deglaze and Simmer:**
    - If using white wine, pour it into the pot and scrape up any browned bits from the bottom. Allow the wine to reduce for about 2 minutes.
    - Add the chicken or vegetable broth, clam juice, bay leaf, thyme, and parsley. Bring to a boil, then reduce the heat and let it simmer until the vegetables are tender, about 15 minutes.
4. **Add Clams and Cream:**

- Stir in the heavy cream and reserved clams. Continue to cook over low heat until heated through, about 5 minutes.

5. **Thicken (Optional):**
    - If you prefer a thicker chowder, you can mix the flour with a bit of water to create a slurry. Stir it into the chowder and cook for an additional 5 minutes until thickened.

6. **Season and Serve:**
    - Taste the chowder and adjust seasoning with salt and pepper as needed. Remove the bay leaf.

7. **Garnish and Enjoy:**
    - Serve the clam chowder hot, garnished with crispy bacon bits and fresh parsley if desired. Accompany with lemon wedges, oyster crackers, or crusty bread for a complete meal.

This Pacific Northwest Clam Chowder is creamy, hearty, and perfect for a cozy meal. Enjoy!

Cedar-Plank Grilled Salmon

Ingredients:

- 1 cedar plank (soaked in water for at least 1 hour)
- 4 salmon fillets (6 oz each)
- 2 tablespoons olive oil
- 2 tablespoons maple syrup or honey
- 2 tablespoons soy sauce
- 2 cloves garlic, minced
- 1 tablespoon Dijon mustard
- 1 teaspoon dried thyme or 1 tablespoon fresh thyme leaves
- 1 teaspoon lemon zest
- 1 tablespoon fresh lemon juice
- Salt and freshly ground black pepper to taste
- Lemon wedges (for serving)
- Fresh parsley or dill (for garnish)

Instructions:

1. **Prepare the Cedar Plank:**
    - Soak the cedar plank in water for at least 1 hour before grilling. This helps prevent it from catching fire on the grill.
2. **Prepare the Marinade:**
    - In a small bowl, whisk together the olive oil, maple syrup (or honey), soy sauce, minced garlic, Dijon mustard, thyme, lemon zest, and lemon juice.
3. **Marinate the Salmon:**
    - Place the salmon fillets in a shallow dish or resealable plastic bag. Pour half of the marinade over the salmon, reserving the other half for basting. Let the salmon marinate in the refrigerator for at least 30 minutes.
4. **Preheat the Grill:**
    - Preheat your grill to medium-high heat.
5. **Prepare the Cedar Plank:**
    - Place the soaked cedar plank on the grill grates and close the lid. Allow it to heat and begin to smoke, about 3-5 minutes.
6. **Grill the Salmon:**
    - Carefully place the marinated salmon fillets on the cedar plank, skin-side down if the skin is still on. Brush the fillets with the reserved marinade.
    - Close the grill lid and cook the salmon for 15-20 minutes, or until the salmon is cooked through and flakes easily with a fork. The cooking time may vary depending on the thickness of the fillets.
7. **Serve:**
    - Remove the cedar plank from the grill and transfer the salmon to a serving platter.
    - Garnish with fresh lemon wedges and chopped parsley or dill.

8. **Enjoy:**
    - Serve the cedar-plank grilled salmon with your favorite side dishes, such as roasted vegetables, rice, or a fresh salad.

This method infuses the salmon with a subtle smoky flavor from the cedar plank, making it a delicious and impressive dish for any occasion. Enjoy your grilled salmon!

Washington Apple Crisp

Ingredients:

- **For the Apple Filling:**
    - 6 cups peeled, cored, and sliced Washington apples (such as Granny Smith, Honeycrisp, or Fuji)
    - 1/2 cup granulated sugar
    - 1 tablespoon lemon juice
    - 1 teaspoon ground cinnamon
    - 1/4 teaspoon ground nutmeg
    - 2 tablespoons all-purpose flour
- **For the Crisp Topping:**
    - 1 cup old-fashioned rolled oats
    - 1/2 cup all-purpose flour
    - 1/2 cup packed brown sugar
    - 1/2 teaspoon ground cinnamon
    - 1/4 teaspoon salt
    - 1/2 cup unsalted butter, cold and cut into small pieces

Instructions:

1. **Preheat Oven:**
    - Preheat your oven to 350°F (175°C).
2. **Prepare the Apple Filling:**
    - In a large mixing bowl, toss the sliced apples with granulated sugar, lemon juice, ground cinnamon, ground nutmeg, and flour until well coated.
3. **Prepare the Crisp Topping:**
    - In another bowl, combine the oats, flour, brown sugar, ground cinnamon, and salt. Add the cold butter pieces.
    - Using a pastry cutter, fork, or your fingers, work the butter into the dry ingredients until the mixture resembles coarse crumbs.
4. **Assemble the Crisp:**
    - Transfer the apple mixture to a 9x13-inch baking dish or an equivalent-sized dish.
    - Evenly sprinkle the crisp topping over the apples.
5. **Bake:**
    - Bake in the preheated oven for 40-45 minutes, or until the topping is golden brown and the apple filling is bubbling and tender.
6. **Cool and Serve:**
    - Allow the apple crisp to cool slightly before serving. It can be served warm or at room temperature.
7. **Optional:**
    - Serve with a scoop of vanilla ice cream or a dollop of whipped cream for extra indulgence.

This Washington Apple Crisp highlights the natural sweetness and tartness of the apples, making it a comforting and satisfying dessert. Enjoy!

Marionberry Pie

Ingredients:

- **For the Pie Crust:**
    - 2 1/2 cups all-purpose flour
    - 1 teaspoon granulated sugar
    - 1 teaspoon salt
    - 1 cup (2 sticks) cold unsalted butter, cut into small cubes
    - 1/4 to 1/2 cup ice water
- **For the Marionberry Filling:**
    - 5 cups fresh or frozen marionberries (if using frozen, thaw and drain them first)
    - 3/4 cup granulated sugar
    - 1/4 cup cornstarch
    - 1/4 teaspoon salt
    - 1 tablespoon lemon juice
    - 1 teaspoon lemon zest
    - 1/2 teaspoon ground cinnamon (optional)
- **For Assembly:**
    - 1 egg, beaten (for egg wash)
    - 1 tablespoon granulated sugar (for sprinkling on top)

Instructions:

1. **Prepare the Pie Crust:**
    - In a large bowl, whisk together the flour, sugar, and salt.
    - Cut in the cold butter using a pastry cutter, fork, or your fingers until the mixture resembles coarse crumbs with pea-sized bits of butter.
    - Gradually add ice water, a tablespoon at a time, until the dough starts to come together. Be careful not to overwork the dough.
    - Divide the dough in half, form each half into a disk, wrap in plastic wrap, and refrigerate for at least 1 hour.
2. **Prepare the Marionberry Filling:**
    - In a large bowl, combine the marionberries, sugar, cornstarch, salt, lemon juice, lemon zest, and cinnamon. Mix gently until the berries are evenly coated. Set aside.
3. **Roll Out the Dough:**
    - On a lightly floured surface, roll out one disk of dough to fit a 9-inch pie dish. Carefully transfer the dough to the pie dish and press it into the bottom and up the sides. Trim any excess dough.
4. **Add the Filling:**
    - Pour the marionberry filling into the prepared pie crust, spreading it evenly.
5. **Top the Pie:**

- Roll out the second disk of dough and place it over the filling. You can either cover the pie with a full sheet of dough and cut a few slits for steam vents or create a lattice pattern with strips of dough.
- Trim and crimp the edges of the dough to seal.
6. **Bake the Pie:**
    - Preheat your oven to 400°F (200°C).
    - Brush the top crust with the beaten egg and sprinkle with granulated sugar.
    - Place the pie on a baking sheet to catch any drips and bake for 45-55 minutes, or until the crust is golden brown and the filling is bubbling.
7. **Cool and Serve:**
    - Allow the pie to cool completely before slicing. This helps the filling set properly.
8. **Optional:**
    - Serve with a scoop of vanilla ice cream or a dollop of whipped cream for extra indulgence.

Enjoy your homemade Marionberry Pie!

Wild Mushroom Risotto

Ingredients:

- 1 pound wild mushrooms (such as porcini, chanterelles, shiitake, or a mix), cleaned and sliced
- 4 tablespoons unsalted butter, divided
- 2 tablespoons olive oil
- 1 small onion, finely chopped
- 2 cloves garlic, minced
- 1 1/2 cups Arborio rice
- 1/2 cup dry white wine
- 4 cups chicken or vegetable broth, warmed
- 1 cup freshly grated Parmesan cheese
- 1/4 cup chopped fresh parsley
- Salt and freshly ground black pepper to taste
- Optional: 1/2 teaspoon truffle oil (for a gourmet touch)

Instructions:

1. **Prepare the Mushrooms:**
   - In a large skillet, heat 2 tablespoons of butter and 2 tablespoons of olive oil over medium heat.
   - Add the sliced mushrooms and cook until they are browned and tender, about 5-7 minutes. Season with a little salt and pepper. Remove the mushrooms from the skillet and set aside.
2. **Sauté Onions and Garlic:**
   - In a large, heavy-bottomed saucepan or Dutch oven, melt 2 tablespoons of butter over medium heat.
   - Add the finely chopped onion and cook until it is translucent and soft, about 3-4 minutes.
   - Stir in the minced garlic and cook for an additional 1 minute.
3. **Cook the Rice:**
   - Add the Arborio rice to the saucepan and stir to coat the rice with the butter and onions. Cook for 2-3 minutes, until the rice is lightly toasted and opaque.
4. **Deglaze with Wine:**
   - Pour in the white wine and cook, stirring frequently, until the wine is mostly absorbed by the rice.
5. **Add Broth:**
   - Begin adding the warm broth, one ladleful at a time, stirring frequently. Allow the rice to absorb the broth before adding more. Continue this process until the rice is creamy and al dente, about 18-20 minutes. You may not need all of the broth.
6. **Incorporate Mushrooms and Cheese:**
   - When the rice is nearly done, stir in the cooked mushrooms and cook for a few more minutes until heated through.

- Remove from heat and stir in the grated Parmesan cheese until melted and well combined.
- Season with salt and freshly ground black pepper to taste.
7. **Finish and Serve:**
    - If using, drizzle with truffle oil for an extra layer of flavor.
    - Garnish with chopped fresh parsley and additional Parmesan cheese if desired.
8. **Enjoy:**
    - Serve the risotto hot, and enjoy the rich, creamy texture and earthy mushroom flavors.

This Wild Mushroom Risotto is a comforting and elegant dish that's perfect for a special occasion or a cozy dinner. Enjoy!

Smoked Steelhead Trout

Ingredients:

- 2 steelhead trout fillets (about 1.5 to 2 pounds each)
- 1/4 cup kosher salt
- 1/4 cup brown sugar
- 1 tablespoon black pepper
- 1 tablespoon smoked paprika
- 1 tablespoon garlic powder
- 1 tablespoon onion powder
- 1 teaspoon dried thyme (optional)
- 1 teaspoon crushed red pepper flakes (optional, for a bit of heat)
- Wood chips for smoking (such as alder or hickory)

Instructions:

1. **Prepare the Brine:**
    - In a small bowl, mix together the kosher salt, brown sugar, black pepper, smoked paprika, garlic powder, onion powder, and any optional spices.
2. **Brine the Fish:**
    - Pat the trout fillets dry with paper towels.
    - Rub the spice mixture evenly over the surface of the fish.
    - Place the fillets in a large resealable plastic bag or shallow dish.
    - Cover and refrigerate for 4 to 6 hours to allow the flavors to penetrate and the fish to firm up.
3. **Rinse and Dry:**
    - After brining, rinse the trout fillets under cold water to remove excess salt and sugar.
    - Pat the fillets dry with paper towels.
    - Place the fillets on a wire rack or a plate and let them air-dry in the refrigerator for 1 to 2 hours. This helps form a pellicle, a tacky surface on the fish that helps it absorb smoke.
4. **Prepare the Smoker:**
    - Preheat your smoker according to the manufacturer's instructions.
    - If using a charcoal grill, set it up for indirect heat and add wood chips to the coals. If using a gas grill, place wood chips in a smoker box or a foil pouch with holes.
5. **Smoke the Trout:**
    - Place the fillets on the smoker grates or a grilling rack.
    - Smoke the trout at 175-200°F (80-93°C) for about 1.5 to 2 hours, or until the fish reaches an internal temperature of 145°F (63°C) and flakes easily with a fork.
6. **Cool and Serve:**
    - Remove the trout from the smoker and let it cool slightly before serving.
    - The smoked trout can be served warm or cold.
7. **Optional Serving Suggestions:**

- Serve with crackers, cream cheese, and fresh herbs for a simple appetizer.
- Flake the smoked trout over salads or pasta dishes for added flavor.

Enjoy the rich, smoky flavor of your homemade smoked steelhead trout!

Apple Cider Braised Pork

Ingredients:

- 3-4 pounds pork shoulder (also called pork butt), cut into 3-inch chunks
- Salt and freshly ground black pepper to taste
- 2 tablespoons vegetable oil
- 1 large onion, chopped
- 2 cloves garlic, minced
- 2 tablespoons tomato paste
- 1 cup apple cider (not vinegar)
- 1 cup chicken broth
- 1/4 cup apple cider vinegar
- 2 tablespoons Dijon mustard
- 2 tablespoons brown sugar
- 1 tablespoon fresh thyme leaves (or 1 teaspoon dried thyme)
- 1 bay leaf
- 4 carrots, peeled and cut into 2-inch pieces
- 3-4 medium potatoes, peeled and cut into chunks (optional)
- 1 tablespoon all-purpose flour (optional, for thickening)

Instructions:

1. **Prepare the Pork:**
   - Season the pork chunks generously with salt and pepper.
2. **Sear the Pork:**
   - Heat vegetable oil in a large Dutch oven or heavy-bottomed pot over medium-high heat.
   - Add the pork chunks in batches, searing on all sides until browned. Transfer the seared pork to a plate and set aside.
3. **Sauté Vegetables:**
   - In the same pot, add the chopped onion and cook until softened, about 5 minutes.
   - Add the minced garlic and cook for an additional 1 minute.
   - Stir in the tomato paste and cook for another 2 minutes to caramelize.
4. **Deglaze and Build the Braising Liquid:**
   - Pour in the apple cider, scraping up any browned bits from the bottom of the pot.
   - Add the chicken broth, apple cider vinegar, Dijon mustard, brown sugar, thyme, and bay leaf. Stir to combine.
5. **Braise the Pork:**
   - Return the seared pork chunks to the pot, making sure they are submerged in the liquid as much as possible.
   - Bring the mixture to a simmer, then cover the pot with a lid and transfer it to a preheated oven at 300°F (150°C).
   - Braise for 2.5 to 3 hours, or until the pork is tender and easily shreds with a fork.
6. **Add Vegetables:**

- About 1 hour before the end of the cooking time, add the carrots and potatoes (if using) to the pot. Stir to combine, and continue to braise until the vegetables are tender.
7. **Thicken the Sauce (Optional):**
    - If you prefer a thicker sauce, remove the pork and vegetables from the pot and set aside.
    - Bring the remaining liquid to a simmer on the stovetop. Mix 1 tablespoon of flour with 2 tablespoons of water to make a slurry and stir it into the simmering liquid. Cook until thickened, about 5 minutes.
8. **Serve:**
    - Return the pork and vegetables to the pot and stir to coat with the sauce.
    - Serve hot, with mashed potatoes, rice, or crusty bread to soak up the delicious sauce.

Enjoy your Apple Cider Braised Pork, a dish full of comforting flavors perfect for a cozy meal!

Columbia River Salmon Steaks

Ingredients:

- 4 salmon steaks (about 1-inch thick)
- 2 tablespoons olive oil
- 2 tablespoons lemon juice
- 2 cloves garlic, minced
- 1 tablespoon fresh rosemary, chopped (or 1 teaspoon dried rosemary)
- 1 tablespoon fresh thyme, chopped (or 1 teaspoon dried thyme)
- 1 teaspoon smoked paprika
- Salt and freshly ground black pepper to taste
- Lemon wedges, for serving
- Fresh herbs, for garnish (optional)

Instructions:

1. **Prepare the Marinade:**
   - In a small bowl, whisk together the olive oil, lemon juice, minced garlic, rosemary, thyme, smoked paprika, salt, and pepper.
2. **Marinate the Salmon:**
   - Place the salmon steaks in a shallow dish or resealable plastic bag. Pour the marinade over the salmon, ensuring each piece is evenly coated.
   - Cover and refrigerate for at least 30 minutes, but no longer than 1 hour.
3. **Preheat the Grill:**
   - Preheat your grill to medium-high heat. If using a charcoal grill, make sure the coals are evenly distributed.
4. **Grill the Salmon Steaks:**
   - Remove the salmon steaks from the marinade and discard the marinade.
   - Lightly oil the grill grates or use a grill pan to prevent sticking.
   - Place the salmon steaks on the grill and cook for about 4-6 minutes per side, depending on the thickness. The salmon should be opaque and flake easily with a fork. Avoid overcooking to maintain the moisture and tenderness of the fish.
5. **Serve:**
   - Remove the salmon steaks from the grill and let them rest for a few minutes.
   - Serve with lemon wedges and garnish with fresh herbs if desired.
6. **Optional:**
   - Pair with your favorite sides, such as roasted vegetables, a fresh salad, or rice.

This recipe for Columbia River Salmon Steaks brings out the best in this prized fish with a simple, fresh marinade that enhances its natural flavor. Enjoy your grilled salmon!

Seattle-Style Hot Dogs

Ingredients:

- **For the Hot Dogs:**
    - 4 beef hot dogs
    - 4 hot dog buns
    - 1 tablespoon vegetable oil (for grilling)
- **For the Toppings:**
    - 1 cup cream cheese, softened
    - 1 cup chopped sauerkraut (drained)
    - 1 cup diced yellow onions
    - 2 tablespoons olive oil
    - 1 tablespoon apple cider vinegar
    - 1 tablespoon brown sugar
    - 1 teaspoon caraway seeds (optional)
    - 1/4 cup chopped fresh parsley (optional, for garnish)
    - 1/4 cup shredded cheddar cheese (optional)

Instructions:

1. **Prepare the Onions:**
    - In a medium skillet, heat the olive oil over medium heat.
    - Add the diced onions and cook until they are soft and golden brown, about 8-10 minutes.
    - Stir in the apple cider vinegar, brown sugar, and caraway seeds (if using). Cook for another 2-3 minutes until the onions are caramelized. Remove from heat.
2. **Prepare the Sauerkraut:**
    - Heat the sauerkraut in a small saucepan over low heat, stirring occasionally, until warmed through. If you prefer, you can add a splash of apple cider vinegar for extra tanginess.
3. **Grill the Hot Dogs:**
    - Preheat your grill to medium-high heat.
    - Lightly oil the grill grates to prevent sticking.
    - Grill the hot dogs, turning occasionally, until they are heated through and have nice grill marks, about 5-7 minutes.
4. **Prepare the Buns:**
    - Cut the hot dog buns in half, but not all the way through, to create a pocket.
    - Optionally, you can lightly toast the buns on the grill for a minute or two until they are golden brown.
5. **Assemble the Hot Dogs:**
    - Spread a generous amount of cream cheese inside each bun.
    - Place a grilled hot dog in each bun.
    - Top with warmed sauerkraut and caramelized onions.
    - Sprinkle with shredded cheddar cheese if desired.
    - Garnish with chopped fresh parsley for a fresh touch.
6. **Serve:**

- Serve your Seattle-style hot dogs with your favorite side dishes, such as fries or a salad.

These Seattle-style hot dogs combine rich, creamy, and tangy flavors, making them a satisfying and unique twist on the traditional hot dog. Enjoy!

Washington Berry Cobbler

Ingredients:

- **For the Berry Filling:**
    - 4 cups mixed fresh berries (such as blueberries, raspberries, blackberries, and/or strawberries, hulled and sliced)
    - 1 cup granulated sugar
    - 2 tablespoons cornstarch
    - 1 tablespoon lemon juice
    - 1 teaspoon vanilla extract
    - 1/4 teaspoon salt
- **For the Cobbler Topping:**
    - 1 1/2 cups all-purpose flour
    - 1/2 cup granulated sugar
    - 2 teaspoons baking powder
    - 1/2 teaspoon salt
    - 1/2 cup unsalted butter, cold and cut into small pieces
    - 1/2 cup milk (whole or 2%)
    - 1 large egg
    - 1 teaspoon vanilla extract
- **For Serving (optional):**
    - Vanilla ice cream or whipped cream

Instructions:

1. **Prepare the Berry Filling:**
    - Preheat your oven to 375°F (190°C).
    - In a large bowl, combine the mixed berries, granulated sugar, cornstarch, lemon juice, vanilla extract, and salt. Stir until the berries are evenly coated.
    - Transfer the berry mixture to a 9x13-inch baking dish or a similar-sized ovenproof dish.
2. **Prepare the Cobbler Topping:**
    - In a medium bowl, whisk together the flour, sugar, baking powder, and salt.
    - Cut the cold butter into the dry ingredients using a pastry cutter, fork, or your fingers until the mixture resembles coarse crumbs.
    - In a separate bowl, whisk together the milk, egg, and vanilla extract.
    - Pour the milk mixture into the flour mixture and stir until just combined. The batter will be thick.
3. **Assemble the Cobbler:**
    - Spoon dollops of the cobbler topping over the berry filling. The topping does not need to cover the berries completely; it will spread out as it bakes.
4. **Bake:**
    - Bake in the preheated oven for 35-45 minutes, or until the topping is golden brown and the berry filling is bubbling.
5. **Cool and Serve:**

- Allow the cobbler to cool for a few minutes before serving. This helps the filling to set up slightly.
6. **Optional:**
    - Serve warm with a scoop of vanilla ice cream or a dollop of whipped cream for extra indulgence.

This Washington Berry Cobbler is a delightful dessert that highlights the fresh, vibrant flavors of local berries. Enjoy!

Roasted Garlic and Herb Chicken

Ingredients:

- **For the Chicken:**
    - 1 whole chicken (about 4-5 pounds)
    - 2 tablespoons olive oil
    - Salt and freshly ground black pepper to taste
    - 1 lemon, quartered
- **For the Garlic and Herb Mixture:**
    - 8 cloves garlic, minced
    - 2 tablespoons fresh rosemary, chopped (or 2 teaspoons dried rosemary)
    - 2 tablespoons fresh thyme, chopped (or 2 teaspoons dried thyme)
    - 1 tablespoon fresh parsley, chopped
    - 1 tablespoon Dijon mustard
    - 1 tablespoon honey
    - 1/4 cup unsalted butter, melted
    - 1 teaspoon lemon zest
    - 1 teaspoon paprika (optional, for added color)
- **For Roasting:**
    - 1 cup chicken broth
    - 1/2 cup white wine (optional)
    - 1 onion, quartered
    - 2-3 carrots, peeled and cut into chunks
    - 2-3 celery stalks, cut into chunks

Instructions:

1. **Prepare the Garlic and Herb Mixture:**
    - In a small bowl, combine the minced garlic, rosemary, thyme, parsley, Dijon mustard, honey, melted butter, lemon zest, and paprika if using. Mix well to form a paste.
2. **Prepare the Chicken:**
    - Preheat your oven to 425°F (220°C).
    - Pat the chicken dry with paper towels. This helps to get crispy skin.
    - Rub the chicken all over with olive oil and season generously with salt and pepper, including inside the cavity.
    - Gently loosen the skin of the chicken by sliding your fingers between the skin and the meat. Be careful not to tear the skin.
3. **Apply the Garlic and Herb Mixture:**
    - Spread the garlic and herb mixture evenly under the skin of the chicken, over the meat. Be sure to get some of the mixture under the skin of the breast and thigh areas for more flavor.
    - Place the lemon quarters inside the cavity of the chicken.
4. **Prepare the Roasting Pan:**

- Place the onion, carrots, and celery in the bottom of a roasting pan or large ovenproof dish. These vegetables will act as a rack for the chicken and add flavor to the drippings.

5. **Roast the Chicken:**
    - Place the chicken, breast side up, on top of the vegetables in the roasting pan.
    - Pour the chicken broth and white wine (if using) around the chicken in the pan.
    - Roast the chicken in the preheated oven for 1.5 to 2 hours, or until the internal temperature reaches 165°F (74°C) in the thickest part of the thigh. The skin should be golden brown and crispy. Baste the chicken occasionally with the pan juices for extra flavor and moisture.
6. **Rest the Chicken:**
    - Remove the chicken from the oven and let it rest for 15-20 minutes before carving. This allows the juices to redistribute throughout the meat.
7. **Serve:**
    - Carve the chicken and serve with the roasted vegetables and any additional side dishes of your choice. The pan juices can be spooned over the chicken for added flavor.

Enjoy your Roasted Garlic and Herb Chicken, a delicious and comforting meal that's perfect for any occasion!

Northwest Seafood Stew

Ingredients:

- **For the Stew Base:**
    - 2 tablespoons olive oil
    - 1 large onion, chopped
    - 2 cloves garlic, minced
    - 1 large carrot, peeled and diced
    - 2 celery stalks, diced
    - 1 cup white wine
    - 4 cups seafood stock or fish stock (you can substitute with chicken broth if needed)
    - 1 can (14.5 ounces) diced tomatoes, with their juice
    - 1 cup heavy cream or half-and-half
    - 1 teaspoon dried thyme
    - 1 teaspoon dried oregano
    - 1 bay leaf
    - Salt and freshly ground black pepper to taste
- **For the Seafood:**
    - 1/2 pound fresh salmon, cut into bite-sized pieces
    - 1/2 pound fresh halibut or cod, cut into bite-sized pieces
    - 1/2 pound shrimp, peeled and deveined
    - 1/2 pound clams, scrubbed (little neck or Manila clams work well)
    - 1/2 pound mussels, scrubbed and debearded
    - 2 tablespoons fresh parsley, chopped (for garnish)
    - 1 lemon, cut into wedges (for serving)
- **Optional:**
    - 1 cup frozen or fresh corn kernels
    - 1-2 potatoes, peeled and diced (for added heartiness)

Instructions:

1. **Prepare the Base:**
    - Heat the olive oil in a large pot or Dutch oven over medium heat.
    - Add the chopped onion, garlic, carrot, and celery. Cook, stirring occasionally, until the vegetables are softened, about 5-7 minutes.
2. **Deglaze and Build the Broth:**
    - Pour in the white wine and cook for 2-3 minutes, allowing it to reduce slightly.
    - Add the seafood stock, diced tomatoes with their juice, heavy cream, thyme, oregano, bay leaf, and a pinch of salt and pepper. Stir well to combine.
3. **Simmer the Stew:**
    - Bring the mixture to a gentle simmer. If using potatoes, add them now. Cook for about 15-20 minutes, until the potatoes (if added) are tender and the flavors have melded.

4. **Add the Seafood:**
    - Add the salmon, halibut, and shrimp to the pot. Cook for 3-4 minutes.
    - Add the clams and mussels. Continue cooking until the seafood is cooked through and the clams and mussels have opened, about 5-7 minutes. Discard any clams or mussels that do not open.
5. **Final Adjustments:**
    - Stir in the fresh parsley and adjust the seasoning with more salt and pepper if needed.
6. **Serve:**
    - Ladle the stew into bowls and serve with lemon wedges on the side.
    - For extra flavor, serve with crusty bread or crackers.

Enjoy your Northwest Seafood Stew, a comforting and savory dish that captures the essence of the Pacific Northwest's rich seafood offerings!

Huckleberry Pancakes

Ingredients:

- **For the Pancake Batter:**
    - 1 1/2 cups all-purpose flour
    - 2 tablespoons granulated sugar
    - 2 teaspoons baking powder
    - 1/2 teaspoon baking soda
    - 1/2 teaspoon salt
    - 1 cup buttermilk
    - 1/2 cup milk (whole or 2%)
    - 2 large eggs
    - 1/4 cup unsalted butter, melted
    - 1 teaspoon vanilla extract
- **For the Huckleberries:**
    - 1 cup fresh or frozen huckleberries (if using frozen, do not thaw)
- **For Serving:**
    - Maple syrup
    - Butter
    - Powdered sugar (optional, for dusting)

Instructions:

1. **Prepare the Pancake Batter:**
    - In a large bowl, whisk together the flour, sugar, baking powder, baking soda, and salt.
    - In another bowl, mix the buttermilk, milk, eggs, melted butter, and vanilla extract until well combined.
    - Pour the wet ingredients into the dry ingredients and stir until just combined. The batter will be a bit lumpy; do not overmix.
2. **Incorporate the Huckleberries:**
    - Gently fold the huckleberries into the batter. If using frozen huckleberries, fold them in carefully to prevent the batter from turning blue.
3. **Cook the Pancakes:**
    - Heat a non-stick griddle or skillet over medium heat. Lightly grease it with butter or cooking spray.
    - Pour about 1/4 cup of batter onto the griddle for each pancake. Cook until bubbles start to form on the surface and the edges look set, about 2-3 minutes.
    - Flip the pancakes and cook for another 1-2 minutes, or until golden brown and cooked through.
4. **Serve:**
    - Keep the pancakes warm in a low oven while you cook the remaining pancakes, or serve immediately.
    - Top with butter, maple syrup, and a dusting of powdered sugar if desired.

Enjoy your homemade huckleberry pancakes, a delightful breakfast that captures the sweet and tangy flavor of huckleberries!

Baked Alaskan Salmon with Dill

Ingredients:

- 4 Alaskan salmon fillets (about 6 ounces each)
- 2 tablespoons olive oil
- 2 tablespoons fresh lemon juice
- 2 cloves garlic, minced
- 1 tablespoon fresh dill, chopped (or 1 teaspoon dried dill)
- 1 teaspoon lemon zest
- 1 teaspoon dried thyme (optional)
- Salt and freshly ground black pepper to taste
- Lemon wedges, for serving
- Fresh dill sprigs, for garnish (optional)

Instructions:

1. **Preheat the Oven:**
   - Preheat your oven to 400°F (200°C).
2. **Prepare the Baking Dish:**
   - Lightly grease a baking dish with olive oil or line it with parchment paper.
3. **Season the Salmon:**
   - Pat the salmon fillets dry with paper towels.
   - In a small bowl, mix together the olive oil, lemon juice, minced garlic, chopped dill, lemon zest, and dried thyme (if using).
   - Brush or drizzle the mixture evenly over the salmon fillets.
   - Season with salt and pepper to taste.
4. **Bake the Salmon:**
   - Place the seasoned salmon fillets in the prepared baking dish.
   - Bake in the preheated oven for 12-15 minutes, or until the salmon is opaque and flakes easily with a fork. The cooking time may vary slightly depending on the thickness of the fillets.
5. **Serve:**
   - Remove the salmon from the oven and let it rest for a couple of minutes.
   - Serve with lemon wedges and garnish with fresh dill sprigs if desired.
6. **Optional:**
   - Pair with your favorite sides, such as roasted vegetables, a fresh salad, or rice.

This Baked Alaskan Salmon with Dill is a light and flavorful dish that's perfect for a quick weeknight dinner or a special occasion. Enjoy!

Sweet Corn and Crab Chowder

Ingredients:

- **For the Chowder:**
    - 2 tablespoons unsalted butter
    - 1 large onion, chopped
    - 2 cloves garlic, minced
    - 2 celery stalks, diced
    - 1 large carrot, peeled and diced
    - 4 cups fresh or frozen corn kernels (about 4 ears of corn, if using fresh)
    - 1 cup diced potatoes (about 1 medium potato)
    - 4 cups chicken or vegetable broth
    - 1 cup heavy cream
    - 1 cup milk (whole or 2%)
    - 1 teaspoon dried thyme
    - 1 bay leaf
    - 1 cup lump crab meat (fresh or canned, drained)
    - Salt and freshly ground black pepper to taste
    - 2 tablespoons fresh parsley, chopped (for garnish)
    - 2 green onions, sliced (for garnish)
    - Optional: a pinch of cayenne pepper or hot sauce (for a bit of heat)

Instructions:

1. **Prepare the Base:**
    - In a large pot or Dutch oven, melt the butter over medium heat.
    - Add the chopped onion, garlic, celery, and carrot. Cook, stirring occasionally, until the vegetables are softened, about 5-7 minutes.
2. **Cook the Chowder:**
    - Add the corn kernels and diced potatoes to the pot. Stir well.
    - Pour in the chicken or vegetable broth and add the thyme and bay leaf. Bring to a boil, then reduce the heat and let it simmer for about 15-20 minutes, or until the potatoes are tender.
3. **Add the Cream:**
    - Stir in the heavy cream and milk. Let the chowder simmer for another 5 minutes, stirring occasionally.
4. **Add the Crab Meat:**
    - Gently fold in the crab meat. Continue to cook for an additional 2-3 minutes, until the crab is heated through. If using, add a pinch of cayenne pepper or a few dashes of hot sauce for a bit of heat. Remove the bay leaf.
5. **Season and Garnish:**
    - Season the chowder with salt and freshly ground black pepper to taste.
    - Garnish with chopped parsley and sliced green onions.
6. **Serve:**

- Ladle the chowder into bowls and serve hot.

This Sweet Corn and Crab Chowder is rich and creamy, with the sweet corn and tender crab meat making it a comforting and indulgent dish. Enjoy!

Blackberry and Apple Sauce

Ingredients:

- 2 cups blackberries (fresh or frozen)
- 2 large apples (such as Granny Smith or Honeycrisp), peeled, cored, and diced
- 1/2 cup granulated sugar (adjust to taste depending on the sweetness of the apples and blackberries)
- 1/4 cup water
- 1 tablespoon lemon juice
- 1 teaspoon lemon zest (optional, for added flavor)
- 1/2 teaspoon ground cinnamon (optional)
- 1/4 teaspoon ground nutmeg (optional)
- 1 tablespoon cornstarch (optional, for thickening)

Instructions:

1. **Prepare the Ingredients:**
   - If using frozen blackberries, thaw them slightly and drain any excess liquid.
   - Peel, core, and dice the apples.
2. **Cook the Fruit:**
   - In a medium saucepan, combine the blackberries, diced apples, sugar, water, and lemon juice.
   - If using, add the lemon zest, cinnamon, and nutmeg. Stir to combine.
3. **Simmer:**
   - Bring the mixture to a simmer over medium heat. Cook, stirring occasionally, for about 15-20 minutes, or until the apples are tender and the blackberries have broken down. The sauce should thicken slightly.
4. **Thicken the Sauce (Optional):**
   - If you prefer a thicker sauce, dissolve the cornstarch in 2 tablespoons of water to make a slurry.
   - Stir the slurry into the simmering sauce and cook for an additional 2-3 minutes, or until the sauce reaches your desired thickness.
5. **Blend (Optional):**
   - For a smoother sauce, use an immersion blender to blend the mixture directly in the pot, or transfer it to a blender and blend in batches. Be careful with hot liquids.
6. **Cool and Store:**
   - Remove the saucepan from heat and let the sauce cool slightly.
   - Transfer the sauce to a jar or airtight container. It can be stored in the refrigerator for up to one week or frozen for up to 3 months.
7. **Serve:**
   - Serve the sauce warm or chilled, as a topping for your favorite breakfast foods or desserts.

This Blackberry and Apple Sauce is a delightful combination of tart blackberries and sweet apples, with a touch of spice if you choose to add it. Enjoy!

Grilled Wild Salmon Tacos

Ingredients:

- **For the Salmon:**
    - 1 lb wild salmon fillets
    - 2 tablespoons olive oil
    - 2 tablespoons lime juice
    - 2 cloves garlic, minced
    - 1 tablespoon smoked paprika
    - 1 teaspoon ground cumin
    - 1 teaspoon chili powder
    - Salt and freshly ground black pepper to taste
- **For the Tacos:**
    - 8 small corn or flour tortillas
    - 1 cup shredded red cabbage
    - 1 cup cherry tomatoes, halved
    - 1 avocado, sliced
    - 1/4 cup fresh cilantro, chopped
    - Lime wedges, for serving
- **For the Cilantro Lime Sauce:**
    - 1/2 cup sour cream or Greek yogurt
    - 1/4 cup mayonnaise
    - 2 tablespoons lime juice
    - 2 tablespoons fresh cilantro, chopped
    - 1 clove garlic, minced
    - Salt and freshly ground black pepper to taste

Instructions:

1. **Marinate the Salmon:**
    - In a small bowl, combine the olive oil, lime juice, minced garlic, smoked paprika, cumin, chili powder, salt, and pepper.
    - Rub the marinade all over the salmon fillets. Let them marinate for at least 15-30 minutes.
2. **Prepare the Cilantro Lime Sauce:**
    - In a bowl, mix together the sour cream (or Greek yogurt), mayonnaise, lime juice, chopped cilantro, minced garlic, salt, and pepper. Adjust seasoning to taste. Refrigerate until ready to use.
3. **Grill the Salmon:**
    - Preheat your grill to medium-high heat.
    - Lightly oil the grill grates to prevent sticking.
    - Place the salmon fillets on the grill, skin-side down if applicable. Grill for about 4-6 minutes per side, or until the salmon is cooked through and flakes easily with a fork. The cooking time will vary based on the thickness of the fillets.

- Remove the salmon from the grill and let it rest for a few minutes before flaking into bite-sized pieces.
4. **Warm the Tortillas:**
   - While the salmon is grilling, warm the tortillas on the grill or in a dry skillet over medium heat until they are pliable and slightly charred.
5. **Assemble the Tacos:**
   - Place the grilled salmon pieces onto the warmed tortillas.
   - Top with shredded red cabbage, cherry tomatoes, avocado slices, and chopped cilantro.
6. **Serve:**
   - Drizzle with the cilantro lime sauce.
   - Serve with lime wedges on the side for extra freshness.

These Grilled Wild Salmon Tacos are bursting with flavor and perfect for a summer meal or a quick weeknight dinner. Enjoy the combination of smoky salmon with fresh, crisp toppings and a zesty sauce!

Washington State BBQ Ribs

Ingredients:

- **For the Ribs:**
    - 2 racks of baby back ribs (about 2.5-3 pounds each)
    - 1 tablespoon olive oil
    - Salt and freshly ground black pepper to taste
- **For the Dry Rub:**
    - 2 tablespoons brown sugar
    - 1 tablespoon smoked paprika
    - 1 tablespoon chili powder
    - 1 teaspoon ground cumin
    - 1 teaspoon garlic powder
    - 1 teaspoon onion powder
    - 1/2 teaspoon ground mustard
    - 1/2 teaspoon cayenne pepper (optional, for heat)
    - 1 teaspoon salt
    - 1/2 teaspoon freshly ground black pepper
- **For the BBQ Sauce:**
    - 1 cup ketchup
    - 1/2 cup apple cider vinegar
    - 1/4 cup brown sugar
    - 1/4 cup honey
    - 2 tablespoons Worcestershire sauce
    - 1 tablespoon soy sauce
    - 1 teaspoon smoked paprika
    - 1 teaspoon garlic powder
    - 1/2 teaspoon onion powder
    - 1/4 teaspoon black pepper
    - 1/4 teaspoon salt

Instructions:

1. **Prepare the Ribs:**
    - Preheat your oven to 300°F (150°C). If using a grill, prepare it for indirect cooking.
    - Remove the membrane from the back of the ribs if it hasn't already been removed. Pat the ribs dry with paper towels.
2. **Apply the Dry Rub:**
    - In a small bowl, mix together the brown sugar, smoked paprika, chili powder, cumin, garlic powder, onion powder, ground mustard, cayenne pepper (if using), salt, and pepper.
    - Rub the spice mixture evenly over both sides of the ribs. Let the ribs sit for about 30 minutes to absorb the flavors.

3. **Cook the Ribs:**
   - **Oven Method:**
     - Place the ribs on a rack in a roasting pan or on a baking sheet lined with aluminum foil.
     - Cover tightly with aluminum foil and bake in the preheated oven for 2.5 to 3 hours, or until the ribs are tender and cooked through.
   - **Grill Method:**
     - Preheat your grill to medium heat.
     - Place the ribs on the grill over indirect heat. Cover the grill and cook for 2.5 to 3 hours, turning occasionally.
4. **Prepare the BBQ Sauce:**
   - In a medium saucepan, combine all the BBQ sauce ingredients.
   - Bring to a simmer over medium heat, stirring frequently. Reduce the heat and let it simmer for about 10-15 minutes, or until the sauce thickens slightly.
5. **Finish the Ribs:**
   - After cooking, remove the ribs from the oven or grill. Brush a generous amount of BBQ sauce over the ribs.
   - If using the oven, return the ribs to the oven, uncovered, and bake for an additional 15-20 minutes, or until the sauce is caramelized.
   - If using the grill, move the ribs over direct heat and grill for an additional 10-15 minutes, turning occasionally and basting with BBQ sauce, until the sauce is sticky and caramelized.
6. **Serve:**
   - Remove the ribs from the heat and let them rest for a few minutes before slicing.
   - Serve with additional BBQ sauce on the side.

Enjoy your Washington State BBQ Ribs with classic sides like coleslaw, baked beans, or cornbread!

Clam Linguine

Ingredients:

- **For the Pasta:**
    - 12 ounces linguine or spaghetti
    - Salt for pasta water
- **For the Clam Sauce:**
    - 2 tablespoons olive oil
    - 4 cloves garlic, minced
    - 1/2 teaspoon red pepper flakes (optional, for heat)
    - 1 cup white wine (such as Sauvignon Blanc or Pinot Grigio)
    - 1 cup low-sodium chicken or seafood broth
    - 2 cans (6.5 ounces each) chopped clams, with juice (or 2 cups fresh clams, cleaned and scrubbed)
    - 1/4 cup fresh parsley, chopped
    - 1 tablespoon fresh lemon juice (about half a lemon)
    - Salt and freshly ground black pepper to taste
    - 2 tablespoons unsalted butter (optional, for richness)
- **For Garnish:**
    - Freshly grated Parmesan cheese (optional)
    - Lemon wedges

Instructions:

1. **Cook the Pasta:**
    - Bring a large pot of salted water to a boil.
    - Add the linguine and cook according to the package instructions until al dente. Reserve 1/2 cup of pasta cooking water, then drain the pasta.
2. **Prepare the Clam Sauce:**
    - While the pasta is cooking, heat the olive oil in a large skillet or sauté pan over medium heat.
    - Add the minced garlic and red pepper flakes (if using). Sauté for about 1 minute, until the garlic is fragrant but not browned.
    - Pour in the white wine and bring to a simmer. Let it cook for about 2-3 minutes to reduce slightly.
    - Add the chicken or seafood broth and continue to simmer for another 2 minutes.
3. **Add the Clams:**
    - If using canned clams, add them along with their juice to the skillet. If using fresh clams, add them to the skillet, cover, and cook for about 5-7 minutes, or until the clams have opened. Discard any clams that do not open.
    - Stir in the fresh parsley and lemon juice. Adjust the seasoning with salt and black pepper. If desired, stir in the butter for added richness.
4. **Combine Pasta and Sauce:**

- Add the drained linguine to the skillet with the clam sauce. Toss to combine, adding a little reserved pasta water if needed to loosen the sauce.
5. **Serve:**
    - Divide the linguine and clam sauce among serving plates.
    - Garnish with freshly grated Parmesan cheese, if desired.
    - Serve with lemon wedges on the side.

This Clam Linguine is a delightful and elegant dish, combining the briny sweetness of clams with a light and savory sauce. Enjoy!

Honey-Glazed Roasted Carrots

Ingredients:

- 1 1/2 pounds carrots (about 6-8 medium carrots), peeled and cut into uniform sticks or rounds
- 2 tablespoons olive oil
- 2 tablespoons honey
- 1 tablespoon balsamic vinegar (optional, for extra depth of flavor)
- 1 teaspoon dried thyme or rosemary (or 1 tablespoon fresh herbs, chopped)
- Salt and freshly ground black pepper to taste
- Fresh parsley or additional herbs for garnish (optional)

Instructions:

1. **Preheat the Oven:**
   - Preheat your oven to 425°F (220°C).
2. **Prepare the Carrots:**
   - Peel the carrots and cut them into uniform sticks or rounds to ensure even cooking.
3. **Make the Glaze:**
   - In a small bowl, whisk together the olive oil, honey, balsamic vinegar (if using), and dried thyme or rosemary. If using fresh herbs, you'll add them later.
4. **Toss the Carrots:**
   - Place the carrot pieces in a large bowl or a resealable plastic bag.
   - Pour the honey glaze over the carrots and toss until they are evenly coated.
5. **Roast the Carrots:**
   - Spread the coated carrots in a single layer on a baking sheet. Avoid overcrowding to ensure even roasting.
   - Season with salt and pepper.
6. **Roasting Time:**
   - Roast in the preheated oven for 25-30 minutes, or until the carrots are tender and caramelized, stirring halfway through to ensure even roasting.
7. **Finish and Garnish:**
   - If using fresh herbs, sprinkle them over the carrots right before serving.
   - Garnish with additional fresh parsley or herbs if desired.
8. **Serve:**
   - Transfer the roasted carrots to a serving dish and enjoy them warm.

These Honey-Glazed Roasted Carrots make a fantastic side dish for any meal, adding a touch of sweetness and a lot of flavor. Enjoy!

Berry-Lemon Muffins

Ingredients:

- **For the Muffins:**
    - 2 1/2 cups all-purpose flour
    - 1 cup granulated sugar
    - 1 tablespoon baking powder
    - 1/2 teaspoon baking soda
    - 1/2 teaspoon salt
    - 1 cup milk (whole or 2%)
    - 1/2 cup unsalted butter, melted
    - 2 large eggs
    - 1 teaspoon vanilla extract
    - Zest of 1 large lemon
    - 1/4 cup fresh lemon juice (about 1 large lemon)
    - 1 1/2 cups mixed berries (such as blueberries, raspberries, or chopped strawberries; fresh or frozen)
- **For the Topping (optional):**
    - 2 tablespoons granulated sugar
    - 1 teaspoon lemon zest

Instructions:

1. **Preheat the Oven:**
    - Preheat your oven to 375°F (190°C).
    - Line a muffin tin with paper liners or lightly grease it.
2. **Prepare the Dry Ingredients:**
    - In a large bowl, whisk together the flour, sugar, baking powder, baking soda, and salt.
3. **Prepare the Wet Ingredients:**
    - In another bowl, mix together the milk, melted butter, eggs, vanilla extract, lemon zest, and lemon juice.
4. **Combine Wet and Dry Ingredients:**
    - Pour the wet ingredients into the dry ingredients and stir until just combined. The batter will be lumpy; do not overmix.
    - Gently fold in the berries.
5. **Fill the Muffin Tin:**
    - Divide the batter evenly among the muffin cups, filling each about 2/3 full.
6. **Add the Topping (optional):**
    - In a small bowl, mix together the granulated sugar and lemon zest.
    - Sprinkle the mixture over the tops of the muffins before baking for a sweet and slightly crispy topping.
7. **Bake the Muffins:**

- Bake in the preheated oven for 20-25 minutes, or until a toothpick inserted into the center comes out clean.
8. **Cool and Serve:**
    - Allow the muffins to cool in the tin for 5 minutes, then transfer to a wire rack to cool completely.

These Berry-Lemon Muffins are a refreshing and tasty treat with a perfect balance of sweet and tangy flavors. Enjoy them fresh out of the oven or at room temperature!

Pacific Northwest Meatloaf

Ingredients:

- **For the Meatloaf:**
    - 1 lb ground beef
    - 1/2 lb ground pork
    - 1 cup mushrooms, finely chopped
    - 1 small onion, finely chopped
    - 2 cloves garlic, minced
    - 1 cup breadcrumbs (preferably whole wheat)
    - 1/2 cup milk
    - 2 large eggs
    - 1/4 cup fresh parsley, chopped
    - 2 tablespoons maple syrup
    - 1 teaspoon dried thyme
    - 1 teaspoon dried rosemary
    - 1 teaspoon salt
    - 1/2 teaspoon freshly ground black pepper
- **For the Glaze:**
    - 1/4 cup ketchup
    - 2 tablespoons maple syrup
    - 1 tablespoon Dijon mustard
    - 1 tablespoon apple cider vinegar

Instructions:

1. **Preheat the Oven:**
    - Preheat your oven to 375°F (190°C).
2. **Prepare the Meatloaf Mixture:**
    - In a large skillet, heat a little oil over medium heat. Add the chopped mushrooms, onion, and garlic. Sauté until the vegetables are softened and the mushrooms release their moisture, about 5-7 minutes. Allow to cool slightly.
    - In a large mixing bowl, combine the ground beef, ground pork, sautéed mushrooms and vegetables, breadcrumbs, milk, eggs, parsley, maple syrup, thyme, rosemary, salt, and pepper. Mix until just combined; avoid overmixing.
3. **Form the Meatloaf:**
    - Transfer the meat mixture to a loaf pan, pressing it down gently to shape it. Alternatively, you can form it into a loaf shape and place it on a lined baking sheet.
4. **Prepare the Glaze:**
    - In a small bowl, mix together the ketchup, maple syrup, Dijon mustard, and apple cider vinegar.
    - Spread the glaze evenly over the top of the meatloaf.
5. **Bake the Meatloaf:**

- Bake in the preheated oven for 60-70 minutes, or until the internal temperature reaches 160°F (71°C) and the meatloaf is cooked through.
- If desired, broil for an additional 2-3 minutes to caramelize the glaze.

6. **Cool and Serve:**
   - Allow the meatloaf to rest for 10 minutes before slicing. This helps it hold its shape and makes it easier to cut.
7. **Optional:**
   - Serve with your favorite sides, such as roasted vegetables, mashed potatoes, or a fresh salad.

This Pacific Northwest Meatloaf brings together classic flavors with a regional twist, making it a hearty and satisfying dish for any occasion. Enjoy!

Mushroom and Swiss Quiche

Ingredients:

- **For the Crust:**
    - 1 1/4 cups all-purpose flour
    - 1/2 teaspoon salt
    - 1/2 cup unsalted butter, cold and cut into small pieces
    - 1/4 cup ice water (more if needed)
- **For the Filling:**
    - 1 tablespoon olive oil
    - 1 cup mushrooms, sliced (such as cremini or button mushrooms)
    - 1/2 cup onion, finely chopped
    - 1 cup shredded Swiss cheese
    - 4 large eggs
    - 1 cup half-and-half or whole milk
    - 1/4 cup heavy cream (optional, for extra richness)
    - 1/2 teaspoon dried thyme or fresh thyme leaves
    - Salt and freshly ground black pepper to taste
    - Fresh parsley for garnish (optional)

Instructions:

1. **Prepare the Crust:**
    - In a mixing bowl, combine the flour and salt.
    - Add the cold butter pieces and use a pastry cutter or your fingers to work the butter into the flour until the mixture resembles coarse crumbs.
    - Gradually add the ice water, stirring with a fork, until the dough begins to come together. Add more water if needed, a tablespoon at a time.
    - Form the dough into a disk, wrap it in plastic wrap, and refrigerate for at least 30 minutes.
2. **Preheat the Oven:**
    - Preheat your oven to 375°F (190°C).
3. **Prepare the Filling:**
    - Heat olive oil in a skillet over medium heat.
    - Add the sliced mushrooms and chopped onion. Sauté until the mushrooms are golden and the onions are softened, about 5-7 minutes. Remove from heat and let cool slightly.
    - In a large bowl, whisk together the eggs, half-and-half (or milk), heavy cream (if using), thyme, salt, and pepper.
4. **Roll Out the Crust:**
    - On a lightly floured surface, roll out the chilled dough to fit a 9-inch pie or quiche pan.

    - Transfer the dough to the pan and press it into the bottom and up the sides. Trim any excess dough hanging over the edges. Prick the bottom of the crust with a fork to prevent bubbling.
5. **Pre-Bake the Crust (Optional):**
    - For a crisper crust, you can pre-bake the crust: Place the pie pan in the preheated oven and bake for 10 minutes. Remove from the oven and let it cool slightly before adding the filling.
6. **Assemble the Quiche:**
    - Spread the sautéed mushrooms and onions evenly over the bottom of the crust.
    - Sprinkle the shredded Swiss cheese over the mushrooms.
    - Pour the egg mixture over the cheese and mushrooms.
7. **Bake the Quiche:**
    - Bake in the preheated oven for 35-45 minutes, or until the quiche is set in the center and lightly golden on top.
    - Let the quiche cool slightly before slicing. This helps it set and makes it easier to cut.
8. **Serve:**
    - Garnish with fresh parsley if desired.
    - Serve warm or at room temperature.

This Mushroom and Swiss Quiche is a comforting and versatile dish that's sure to please. Enjoy!

Huckleberry Jam

Ingredients:

- 4 cups fresh huckleberries (or frozen, thawed)
- 2 cups granulated sugar
- 1/4 cup lemon juice (about 2 large lemons)
- 1 package (1.75 oz) fruit pectin (such as Sure-Jell or Ball)
- 1/2 teaspoon unsalted butter (optional, to reduce foaming)

Instructions:

1. **Prepare Jars and Lids:**
   - Sterilize canning jars and lids by placing them in a boiling water bath for 10 minutes or running them through a dishwasher cycle. Keep them hot until ready to use.
2. **Prepare the Huckleberries:**
   - If using fresh huckleberries, rinse them and remove any stems. If using frozen huckleberries, thaw them and drain any excess liquid.
3. **Cook the Jam:**
   - In a large saucepan, combine the huckleberries and lemon juice.
   - Use a potato masher or fork to crush the huckleberries slightly, releasing their juices.
   - Stir in the fruit pectin and bring the mixture to a boil over medium-high heat, stirring constantly.
4. **Add the Sugar:**
   - Once the mixture reaches a rolling boil, add the granulated sugar all at once.
   - Continue to stir constantly and bring the mixture back to a rolling boil. Boil for 1-2 minutes, or until the mixture reaches the gel stage.
5. **Check for Set:**
   - To test if the jam has set, place a small spoonful on a cold plate and let it sit for 1 minute. Run your finger through the center of the jam; if it wrinkles and holds its shape, it's ready. If not, continue boiling for another minute and test again.
6. **Add Butter (Optional):**
   - If desired, stir in 1/2 teaspoon of unsalted butter to reduce foam on the surface.
7. **Fill Jars:**
   - Ladle the hot jam into the prepared sterilized jars, leaving about 1/4-inch headspace at the top.
   - Wipe the rims of the jars with a clean, damp cloth to remove any residue.
8. **Seal the Jars:**
   - Place the sterilized lids on the jars and screw on the metal bands until they are fingertip-tight.
   - Process the jars in a boiling water bath for 5-10 minutes to ensure they are sealed properly.
9. **Cool and Store:**

- Remove the jars from the water bath and let them cool completely on a clean kitchen towel or cooling rack.
- Once cooled, check that the lids have sealed by pressing in the center of each lid. If it doesn't pop back, the jar did not seal properly and should be refrigerated and used soon.

10. **Label and Store:**
    - Label the jars with the date and store them in a cool, dark place. Properly processed and sealed jars can be stored for up to one year.

Enjoy your homemade huckleberry jam on toast, as a filling for pastries, or as a sweet topping for your favorite desserts!

Roasted Beet Salad with Goat Cheese

Ingredients:

- **For the Salad:**
    - 4 medium beets (red or golden, or a mix), trimmed and scrubbed
    - 2 tablespoons olive oil
    - Salt and freshly ground black pepper to taste
    - 4 cups mixed salad greens (such as arugula, spinach, and/or baby greens)
    - 1/2 cup crumbled goat cheese
    - 1/4 cup toasted pecans or walnuts (optional)
    - 1/4 cup thinly sliced red onion (optional)
    - Fresh herbs for garnish (such as parsley or chives, optional)
- **For the Vinaigrette:**
    - 3 tablespoons olive oil
    - 2 tablespoons balsamic vinegar
    - 1 tablespoon honey or maple syrup
    - 1 teaspoon Dijon mustard
    - 1 clove garlic, minced
    - Salt and freshly ground black pepper to taste

Instructions:

1. **Roast the Beets:**
    - Preheat your oven to 400°F (200°C).
    - Wrap each beet individually in aluminum foil and place them on a baking sheet.
    - Roast in the preheated oven for 45-60 minutes, or until the beets are tender when pierced with a fork. The cooking time will vary depending on the size of the beets.
    - Let the beets cool slightly, then peel off the skins (they should come off easily) and cut them into bite-sized pieces.
2. **Prepare the Vinaigrette:**
    - In a small bowl or jar, whisk together the olive oil, balsamic vinegar, honey or maple syrup, Dijon mustard, minced garlic, salt, and pepper until well combined.
3. **Assemble the Salad:**
    - In a large salad bowl, toss the mixed greens with a little of the vinaigrette to lightly coat the leaves.
    - Arrange the roasted beet pieces over the greens.
    - Sprinkle the crumbled goat cheese over the top.
    - Add the toasted pecans or walnuts and sliced red onion, if using.
4. **Dress and Serve:**
    - Drizzle the remaining vinaigrette over the salad just before serving.
    - Garnish with fresh herbs if desired.
5. **Serve:**
    - Toss gently to combine or serve as individual portions.

This Roasted Beet Salad with Goat Cheese is a delightful combination of flavors and textures, making it a perfect side dish or light main course. Enjoy the vibrant colors and delicious taste!

Salmon and Asparagus Foil Packets

Ingredients:

- 4 salmon fillets (about 6 ounces each)
- 1 bunch of asparagus, trimmed and cut into 2-inch pieces
- 2 tablespoons olive oil
- 2 cloves garlic, minced
- 1 lemon, thinly sliced
- 1 teaspoon dried oregano or thyme (or 1 tablespoon fresh, chopped)
- Salt and freshly ground black pepper to taste
- 1/4 cup grated Parmesan cheese (optional)
- Fresh parsley or dill for garnish (optional)

Instructions:

1. **Preheat the Oven:**
   - Preheat your oven to 400°F (200°C). Alternatively, you can cook these packets on the grill.
2. **Prepare the Foil Packets:**
   - Cut four large sheets of aluminum foil, about 12 inches long each.
   - Brush each sheet lightly with olive oil to prevent sticking.
3. **Assemble the Packets:**
   - Place one salmon fillet in the center of each piece of foil.
   - Arrange a portion of asparagus around each salmon fillet.
   - Drizzle with olive oil and sprinkle with minced garlic, dried oregano or thyme, salt, and black pepper.
   - Place a few lemon slices on top of each salmon fillet.
   - If using, sprinkle the grated Parmesan cheese over the top of the salmon and asparagus.
4. **Seal the Packets:**
   - Fold the sides of the foil over the salmon and asparagus, then fold the ends to seal the packet tightly. Make sure the packets are well-sealed to retain moisture.
5. **Cook the Packets:**
   - **Oven Method:** Place the foil packets on a baking sheet and bake in the preheated oven for 15-20 minutes, or until the salmon is cooked through and flakes easily with a fork.
   - **Grill Method:** Preheat the grill to medium-high heat. Place the foil packets on the grill and cook for 15-20 minutes, turning occasionally, until the salmon is cooked through.
6. **Serve:**
   - Carefully open the foil packets (watch out for steam) and transfer the contents to plates.
   - Garnish with fresh parsley or dill if desired.

These Salmon and Asparagus Foil Packets are not only convenient but also packed with flavor. Enjoy this easy, healthy meal with minimal cleanup!

Cherry-Limeade

Ingredients:

- **For the Cherry Syrup:**
    - 2 cups fresh or frozen cherries, pitted
    - 1 cup granulated sugar
    - 1 cup water
    - 1 tablespoon fresh lemon juice (optional, for added brightness)
- **For the Limeade:**
    - 1 cup freshly squeezed lime juice (about 6-8 limes)
    - 4 cups cold water
    - 1/2 cup granulated sugar (adjust to taste)
    - Ice
    - Lime slices and fresh cherries for garnish (optional)

Instructions:

1. **Make the Cherry Syrup:**
    - In a medium saucepan, combine the cherries, sugar, and water.
    - Bring to a boil over medium heat, stirring occasionally to dissolve the sugar.
    - Reduce the heat and let the mixture simmer for about 10 minutes, or until the cherries are soft and the syrup has thickened slightly.
    - Use a spoon or potato masher to gently mash the cherries, releasing more juice.
    - Remove from heat and let the syrup cool.
    - Optionally, stir in the lemon juice for added brightness.
2. **Prepare the Limeade:**
    - In a large pitcher, combine the freshly squeezed lime juice and sugar. Stir until the sugar is fully dissolved.
    - Add the cold water and stir well.
    - Taste and adjust the sweetness if needed by adding more sugar or water.
3. **Combine and Serve:**
    - To serve, pour the limeade into glasses filled with ice.
    - Stir in a few tablespoons of the cherry syrup to each glass, adjusting to your taste. You can also mix the syrup into the entire pitcher if you prefer a more uniform flavor.
    - Garnish with lime slices and fresh cherries if desired.
4. **Chill:**
    - For best results, chill the limeade and cherry syrup in the refrigerator before serving. This will keep your drink cool and refreshing.

Enjoy your homemade Cherry-Limeade—it's the perfect balance of tart and sweet with a vibrant cherry flavor!

Washington State-style Pot Roast

Ingredients:

- **For the Pot Roast:**
    - 3-4 pounds beef chuck roast (or a similar cut like brisket)
    - 2 tablespoons olive oil
    - Salt and freshly ground black pepper to taste
    - 1 large onion, chopped
    - 3 cloves garlic, minced
    - 4 carrots, peeled and cut into large chunks
    - 3-4 Yukon Gold or red potatoes, cut into large chunks
    - 2 cups beef broth
    - 1 cup red wine (optional; can substitute with additional beef broth)
    - 2 tablespoons tomato paste
    - 1 tablespoon Worcestershire sauce
    - 2 teaspoons dried thyme or 1 tablespoon fresh thyme leaves
    - 2 teaspoons dried rosemary or 1 tablespoon fresh rosemary leaves
    - 1 bay leaf
    - 1 cup frozen peas (optional, for added color and flavor)
- **For Garnish:**
    - Fresh parsley, chopped (optional)

Instructions:

1. **Prepare the Roast:**
    - Preheat your oven to 325°F (165°C).
    - Pat the roast dry with paper towels and season generously with salt and pepper.
2. **Sear the Roast:**
    - In a large oven-safe Dutch oven or heavy-bottomed pot, heat the olive oil over medium-high heat.
    - Add the roast and sear on all sides until browned, about 4-5 minutes per side. This step helps to lock in the flavors.
3. **Sauté Vegetables:**
    - Remove the roast from the pot and set aside.
    - In the same pot, add the chopped onion and cook for about 3 minutes, until softened.
    - Add the minced garlic and cook for another minute, stirring frequently.
4. **Deglaze and Build the Sauce:**
    - Stir in the tomato paste and cook for 1-2 minutes.
    - Pour in the red wine (if using) and beef broth, scraping up any browned bits from the bottom of the pot.
    - Stir in the Worcestershire sauce, thyme, rosemary, and bay leaf.
5. **Add Vegetables and Roast:**
    - Return the seared roast to the pot.

- Add the carrots and potatoes around the roast, making sure they are nestled in the liquid.
6. **Cook the Roast:**
   - Cover the pot with a lid and transfer it to the preheated oven.
   - Roast for about 3-4 hours, or until the meat is fork-tender and easily shreds. Cooking time may vary depending on the size of the roast.
7. **Add Peas (Optional):**
   - About 30 minutes before the roast is done, stir in the frozen peas if using.
8. **Finish and Serve:**
   - Once the roast is done, remove it from the pot and let it rest for 10-15 minutes before slicing or shredding.
   - Remove the bay leaf from the sauce.
   - Taste the sauce and adjust seasoning if necessary.
9. **Garnish:**
   - Serve the pot roast with the vegetables and sauce spooned over the top.
   - Garnish with freshly chopped parsley if desired.

This Washington State-style Pot Roast offers a comforting, hearty meal that makes great use of local ingredients and seasonal flavors. Enjoy!

Apple and Sausage Stuffing

Ingredients:

- **For the Stuffing:**
    - 1 pound Italian sausage (bulk, not in casings)
    - 1 tablespoon olive oil
    - 1 large onion, diced
    - 2 celery stalks, diced
    - 2 cloves garlic, minced
    - 2 large apples, peeled, cored, and diced (such as Granny Smith or Honeycrisp)
    - 1/2 cup dried cranberries or raisins
    - 8 cups cubed day-old bread (such as French or Italian bread)
    - 1 cup chicken or vegetable broth (more if needed)
    - 2 large eggs, beaten
    - 1 teaspoon dried sage (or 1 tablespoon fresh sage, chopped)
    - 1 teaspoon dried thyme (or 1 tablespoon fresh thyme, chopped)
    - 1/2 teaspoon dried rosemary (or 1 teaspoon fresh rosemary, chopped)
    - Salt and freshly ground black pepper to taste
    - 2 tablespoons fresh parsley, chopped (optional, for garnish)

Instructions:

1. **Preheat Oven:**
    - Preheat your oven to 350°F (175°C).
2. **Cook the Sausage:**
    - In a large skillet, cook the sausage over medium heat, breaking it into small pieces with a spoon until browned and cooked through. Remove the sausage from the skillet and set aside, leaving some drippings in the pan.
3. **Sauté Vegetables:**
    - In the same skillet, add olive oil if needed. Sauté the onion and celery over medium heat until softened, about 5-7 minutes.
    - Add the garlic and cook for an additional minute until fragrant.
4. **Add Apples and Cranberries:**
    - Stir in the diced apples and dried cranberries. Cook for another 5 minutes, until the apples start to soften.
5. **Combine Ingredients:**
    - In a large mixing bowl, combine the cubed bread with the cooked sausage and vegetable mixture.
    - Add the beaten eggs, herbs (sage, thyme, rosemary), salt, and pepper. Stir to combine.
    - Gradually add the chicken or vegetable broth, a little at a time, until the bread is slightly moist but not soggy. You might need a bit more or less broth depending on the dryness of the bread.
6. **Transfer and Bake:**

- Transfer the stuffing mixture to a greased 9x13-inch baking dish.
- Cover with aluminum foil and bake in the preheated oven for 30 minutes.

7. **Crisp the Top:**
    - After 30 minutes, remove the foil and bake for an additional 15-20 minutes, or until the top is golden brown and crispy.
8. **Garnish and Serve:**
    - Remove from the oven and let cool slightly before serving.
    - Garnish with fresh parsley if desired.

This Apple and Sausage Stuffing is a wonderful combination of savory and sweet flavors, making it a perfect side dish for any holiday meal or special occasion. Enjoy!

Lemon and Herb Grilled Chicken

Ingredients:

- **For the Marinade:**
    - 1/4 cup olive oil
    - 1/4 cup freshly squeezed lemon juice (about 2 lemons)
    - 2 tablespoons lemon zest
    - 4 cloves garlic, minced
    - 2 tablespoons fresh rosemary, chopped (or 1 tablespoon dried rosemary)
    - 2 tablespoons fresh thyme, chopped (or 1 tablespoon dried thyme)
    - 1 tablespoon fresh parsley, chopped (optional)
    - 1 tablespoon Dijon mustard
    - 1 teaspoon honey (optional, for a touch of sweetness)
    - Salt and freshly ground black pepper to taste
- **For the Chicken:**
    - 4 boneless, skinless chicken breasts or 6-8 chicken thighs (bone-in or boneless)
    - Lemon wedges and additional fresh herbs for garnish (optional)

Instructions:

1. **Prepare the Marinade:**
    - In a medium bowl, whisk together the olive oil, lemon juice, lemon zest, minced garlic, rosemary, thyme, parsley (if using), Dijon mustard, honey (if using), salt, and pepper.
2. **Marinate the Chicken:**
    - Place the chicken breasts or thighs in a large resealable plastic bag or a shallow dish.
    - Pour the marinade over the chicken, ensuring all pieces are well coated.
    - Seal the bag or cover the dish and refrigerate for at least 1 hour, or up to 8 hours for more intense flavor.
3. **Preheat the Grill:**
    - Preheat your grill to medium-high heat (about 375°F to 400°F or 190°C to 200°C).
4. **Grill the Chicken:**
    - Remove the chicken from the marinade and discard the marinade.
    - Place the chicken on the grill and cook for 6-8 minutes per side, or until the internal temperature reaches 165°F (74°C) and the chicken is cooked through. The exact cooking time will depend on the thickness of the chicken pieces.
5. **Rest and Garnish:**
    - Remove the chicken from the grill and let it rest for 5 minutes before serving. This helps the juices redistribute and keeps the chicken moist.
    - Garnish with lemon wedges and additional fresh herbs if desired.
6. **Serve:**

- Serve the Lemon and Herb Grilled Chicken with your favorite sides, such as a fresh salad, roasted vegetables, or rice.

This Lemon and Herb Grilled Chicken is light, zesty, and full of flavor, making it a perfect choice for a healthy and satisfying meal. Enjoy!

Wild Mushroom and Barley Soup

Ingredients:

- **For the Soup:**
    - 2 tablespoons olive oil
    - 1 large onion, diced
    - 2 cloves garlic, minced
    - 2 carrots, peeled and diced
    - 2 celery stalks, diced
    - 1 pound mixed wild mushrooms (such as cremini, shiitake, oyster, or chanterelle), cleaned and sliced
    - 1 cup pearl barley
    - 6 cups vegetable broth (or chicken broth)
    - 1 cup dry white wine (optional, can substitute with additional broth)
    - 1 teaspoon dried thyme
    - 1 teaspoon dried rosemary
    - 1 bay leaf
    - Salt and freshly ground black pepper to taste
    - 2 tablespoons soy sauce (optional, for added depth of flavor)
    - 2 tablespoons fresh parsley, chopped (optional, for garnish)

Instructions:

1. **Sauté Vegetables:**
    - Heat olive oil in a large pot or Dutch oven over medium heat.
    - Add the diced onion, carrots, and celery. Sauté until the vegetables are softened, about 5-7 minutes.
    - Stir in the minced garlic and cook for another minute until fragrant.
2. **Cook the Mushrooms:**
    - Add the sliced mushrooms to the pot and cook for 5-7 minutes, until they are browned and have released their moisture.
3. **Add Barley and Broth:**
    - Stir in the pearl barley and cook for 1-2 minutes, allowing it to lightly toast.
    - Pour in the vegetable broth and white wine (if using). Add the dried thyme, rosemary, bay leaf, salt, and pepper.
4. **Simmer the Soup:**
    - Bring the soup to a boil, then reduce the heat to low and cover.
    - Simmer for 30-40 minutes, or until the barley is tender and has absorbed some of the broth. Stir occasionally.
5. **Adjust Seasonings:**
    - If using, stir in the soy sauce for added depth of flavor.
    - Taste and adjust seasoning with more salt and pepper if needed.
6. **Serve:**
    - Remove the bay leaf before serving.

- Ladle the soup into bowls and garnish with freshly chopped parsley if desired.

This Wild Mushroom and Barley Soup is rich, comforting, and packed with deep, savory flavors. It makes for a perfect meal on a chilly day or as a satisfying start to a dinner. Enjoy!

Roasted Brussels Sprouts with Bacon

Ingredients:

- 1 1/2 pounds Brussels sprouts, trimmed and halved
- 6 slices bacon, chopped
- 2 tablespoons olive oil
- 2 cloves garlic, minced
- Salt and freshly ground black pepper to taste
- 1 tablespoon balsamic vinegar (optional, for added flavor)
- 1/4 cup grated Parmesan cheese (optional, for extra flavor)
- Fresh parsley, chopped (optional, for garnish)

Instructions:

1. **Preheat Oven:**
   - Preheat your oven to 400°F (200°C).
2. **Prepare Brussels Sprouts:**
   - Trim the ends of the Brussels sprouts and cut them in half lengthwise.
3. **Cook Bacon:**
   - In a large skillet over medium heat, cook the chopped bacon until crispy. Remove the bacon with a slotted spoon and transfer it to a paper towel-lined plate to drain. Leave about 1 tablespoon of bacon fat in the skillet.
4. **Toss and Roast:**
   - In a large bowl, toss the Brussels sprouts with the olive oil, minced garlic, and a pinch of salt and pepper.
   - Spread the Brussels sprouts on a large baking sheet in a single layer.
   - Roast in the preheated oven for 20-25 minutes, or until the Brussels sprouts are golden brown and crispy on the edges, tossing halfway through for even cooking.
5. **Add Bacon and Finish:**
   - Remove the Brussels sprouts from the oven and toss them with the cooked bacon.
   - If using, drizzle with balsamic vinegar and sprinkle with grated Parmesan cheese while still warm.
6. **Garnish and Serve:**
   - Garnish with chopped fresh parsley if desired.

These Roasted Brussels Sprouts with Bacon are a flavorful and easy-to-make side dish that pairs well with a variety of main courses. Enjoy the crispy, savory combination!

Northwest Berry Smoothie

Ingredients:

- 1 cup fresh or frozen blueberries
- 1 cup fresh or frozen raspberries
- 1 cup fresh or frozen blackberries
- 1 banana, peeled and sliced
- 1 cup plain or vanilla yogurt (Greek or regular)
- 1/2 cup milk (or any non-dairy milk like almond, soy, or oat)
- 1-2 tablespoons honey or maple syrup (optional, for added sweetness)
- 1/2 teaspoon vanilla extract (optional)
- Ice cubes (optional, if using fresh berries)

Instructions:

1. **Prepare the Ingredients:**
   - If using fresh berries, rinse them under cold water and pat them dry. If using frozen berries, no need to thaw them.
   - Slice the banana.
2. **Blend the Smoothie:**
   - In a blender, combine the blueberries, raspberries, blackberries, banana, yogurt, and milk.
   - If desired, add honey or maple syrup for sweetness and vanilla extract for extra flavor.
   - Blend on high until smooth. If the smoothie is too thick, add more milk to reach your desired consistency.
3. **Add Ice (Optional):**
   - If you prefer a colder or thicker smoothie and are using fresh berries, add a handful of ice cubes and blend again until well combined.
4. **Serve:**
   - Pour the smoothie into glasses and serve immediately.
5. **Garnish (Optional):**
   - Garnish with a few fresh berries or a sprig of mint if desired.

This Northwest Berry Smoothie is a delicious and healthy way to enjoy the rich flavors of Pacific Northwest berries. It's perfect for breakfast, a snack, or a refreshing treat anytime!

Washington Apple Salad

Ingredients:

- **For the Salad:**
    - 4 cups mixed salad greens (such as spinach, arugula, or baby greens)
    - 2-3 medium Washington apples (such as Honeycrisp, Fuji, or Gala), cored and thinly sliced
    - 1/2 cup walnuts or pecans, toasted
    - 1/2 cup crumbled blue cheese or feta cheese
    - 1/4 cup dried cranberries or raisins
    - 1/4 red onion, thinly sliced (optional)
- **For the Dressing:**
    - 1/4 cup extra-virgin olive oil
    - 2 tablespoons apple cider vinegar
    - 1 tablespoon honey or maple syrup
    - 1 teaspoon Dijon mustard
    - Salt and freshly ground black pepper to taste

Instructions:

1. **Prepare the Salad Ingredients:**
    - In a large salad bowl, combine the mixed greens with the sliced apples.
    - Add the toasted walnuts or pecans, crumbled cheese, dried cranberries, and thinly sliced red onion (if using).
2. **Make the Dressing:**
    - In a small bowl or jar, whisk together the olive oil, apple cider vinegar, honey or maple syrup, Dijon mustard, salt, and pepper until well combined.
3. **Assemble the Salad:**
    - Drizzle the dressing over the salad and toss gently to coat all the ingredients.
4. **Serve:**
    - Serve the salad immediately, or refrigerate the dressing separately until ready to serve to keep the greens crisp.

This Washington Apple Salad is a delightful combination of sweet apples, crunchy nuts, and tangy cheese, all brought together with a light and flavorful dressing. It's perfect as a side dish or a light main course. Enjoy!

Salmon and Potato Chowder

Ingredients:

- **For the Chowder:**
    - 2 tablespoons olive oil or butter
    - 1 large onion, diced
    - 2 cloves garlic, minced
    - 2 carrots, peeled and diced
    - 2 celery stalks, diced
    - 4 cups peeled and diced potatoes (such as Yukon Gold or Russet)
    - 4 cups chicken or vegetable broth
    - 1 cup heavy cream or half-and-half
    - 1 pound salmon fillet, skinless and boneless, cut into bite-sized pieces
    - 1 cup frozen corn (optional)
    - 1 teaspoon dried thyme or 1 tablespoon fresh thyme, chopped
    - 1 bay leaf
    - Salt and freshly ground black pepper to taste
    - 2 tablespoons fresh parsley or chives, chopped (optional, for garnish)

Instructions:

1. **Sauté Vegetables:**
    - In a large pot or Dutch oven, heat the olive oil or butter over medium heat.
    - Add the diced onion, carrots, and celery. Sauté until the vegetables are softened, about 5-7 minutes.
    - Add the minced garlic and cook for another minute.
2. **Cook the Potatoes:**
    - Stir in the diced potatoes and cook for another 2 minutes.
    - Add the chicken or vegetable broth and bay leaf. Bring the mixture to a boil.
3. **Simmer the Chowder:**
    - Reduce the heat to low and simmer for about 15-20 minutes, or until the potatoes are tender.
4. **Add Salmon and Cream:**
    - Stir in the heavy cream or half-and-half, and add the salmon pieces.
    - Cook for an additional 5-7 minutes, or until the salmon is cooked through and flakes easily with a fork.
5. **Add Optional Ingredients:**
    - If using, add the frozen corn and stir to combine. Cook for another 2-3 minutes, until the corn is heated through.
6. **Season and Garnish:**
    - Remove the bay leaf from the chowder.
    - Stir in the dried or fresh thyme, and season with salt and freshly ground black pepper to taste.
    - Garnish with fresh parsley or chives if desired.

7. **Serve:**
    - Ladle the chowder into bowls and serve hot with crusty bread or crackers.

This Salmon and Potato Chowder is rich, creamy, and packed with flavor, making it a comforting choice for a satisfying meal. Enjoy!

Blackberry Crumble Bars

Ingredients:

- **For the Crust and Topping:**
    - 1 1/2 cups all-purpose flour
    - 1/2 cup granulated sugar
    - 1/2 teaspoon baking powder
    - 1/4 teaspoon salt
    - 1/2 cup unsalted butter, cold and cut into small pieces
    - 1/2 cup old-fashioned oats
- **For the Blackberry Filling:**
    - 2 cups fresh or frozen blackberries (if using frozen, do not thaw)
    - 1/2 cup granulated sugar
    - 2 tablespoons cornstarch
    - 1 tablespoon lemon juice
    - 1 teaspoon lemon zest
    - 1/2 teaspoon vanilla extract

Instructions:

1. **Preheat Oven:**
    - Preheat your oven to 350°F (175°C). Grease or line an 8x8-inch baking dish with parchment paper.
2. **Prepare the Crust and Topping:**
    - In a medium bowl, whisk together the flour, sugar, baking powder, and salt.
    - Cut in the cold butter using a pastry cutter, fork, or your fingers until the mixture resembles coarse crumbs.
    - Stir in the oats.
    - Reserve 1 cup of the mixture for the topping. Press the remaining mixture evenly into the bottom of the prepared baking dish to form the crust.
3. **Prepare the Blackberry Filling:**
    - In a medium saucepan, combine the blackberries, sugar, cornstarch, lemon juice, lemon zest, and vanilla extract.
    - Cook over medium heat, stirring frequently, until the mixture starts to thicken and bubble, about 5-7 minutes.
    - Remove from heat and let it cool slightly.
4. **Assemble the Bars:**
    - Spread the blackberry filling evenly over the prepared crust.
    - Sprinkle the reserved crumble mixture evenly over the top of the blackberry filling.
5. **Bake:**
    - Bake in the preheated oven for 35-40 minutes, or until the topping is golden brown and the filling is bubbly.
6. **Cool and Cut:**

- Allow the bars to cool completely in the baking dish on a wire rack.
- Once cooled, cut into squares or rectangles.
7. **Serve:**
   - Serve as a snack, dessert, or with a scoop of vanilla ice cream or a dollop of whipped cream.

These Blackberry Crumble Bars are a delightful blend of sweet and tart with a satisfying crumbly topping. Enjoy!

Pan-Seared Dungeness Crab

Ingredients:

- 1-2 Dungeness crabs, pre-cooked (or fresh if you're cooking them yourself) - about 1.5-2 pounds each
- 2 tablespoons olive oil or unsalted butter
- 2 cloves garlic, minced
- 1 tablespoon fresh lemon juice
- 1 teaspoon lemon zest
- 1 tablespoon fresh parsley, chopped
- Salt and freshly ground black pepper to taste
- Lemon wedges, for serving

Instructions:

1. **Prepare the Crab:**
    - If using pre-cooked crabs, clean and crack them. If using live crabs, cook them in boiling water for 10-15 minutes, then cool and clean them.
2. **Heat the Pan:**
    - Heat the olive oil or butter in a large skillet over medium-high heat.
3. **Sear the Crab:**
    - Add the crab pieces to the hot skillet. If the crab pieces are large, you may need to do this in batches to avoid overcrowding.
    - Sear the crab pieces for about 3-4 minutes per side, or until they are heated through and have developed a golden-brown crust.
4. **Add Flavor:**
    - In the last minute of cooking, add the minced garlic to the pan and stir it around to avoid burning.
    - Drizzle the fresh lemon juice over the crab and sprinkle with lemon zest.
5. **Season:**
    - Season with salt and freshly ground black pepper to taste.
    - Add chopped fresh parsley and give everything a final toss.
6. **Serve:**
    - Transfer the crab pieces to a serving platter.
    - Serve with lemon wedges on the side for additional brightness.

This Pan-Seared Dungeness Crab is wonderfully simple and highlights the natural sweetness of the crab. It's perfect as a main course or a special appetizer. Enjoy!

Herb-Crusted Roasted Chicken

Ingredients:

- 1 whole chicken (about 4-5 pounds), patted dry
- 2 tablespoons olive oil
- 1 tablespoon fresh rosemary, chopped (or 1 teaspoon dried rosemary)
- 1 tablespoon fresh thyme, chopped (or 1 teaspoon dried thyme)
- 1 tablespoon fresh parsley, chopped
- 2 cloves garlic, minced
- 1 lemon, quartered
- Salt and freshly ground black pepper to taste
- 1/2 cup chicken broth (or white wine)

Instructions:

1. **Preheat Oven:**
    - Preheat your oven to 425°F (220°C).
2. **Prepare the Herb Mixture:**
    - In a small bowl, mix together the olive oil, chopped rosemary, thyme, parsley, and minced garlic.
3. **Season the Chicken:**
    - Place the chicken in a roasting pan or on a rack set over a baking sheet.
    - Rub the herb mixture all over the chicken, making sure to get some under the skin where possible for maximum flavor.
    - Season the chicken generously with salt and freshly ground black pepper, including inside the cavity.
4. **Add Lemon and Roast:**
    - Stuff the quartered lemon into the cavity of the chicken.
    - Pour the chicken broth or white wine into the bottom of the roasting pan to keep the chicken moist and add flavor.
5. **Roast the Chicken:**
    - Roast the chicken in the preheated oven for about 1 hour to 1 hour and 15 minutes, or until the internal temperature reaches 165°F (74°C) when measured in the thickest part of the thigh. Baste the chicken occasionally with the pan juices to keep it moist and golden brown.
    - If the skin is browning too quickly, cover the chicken loosely with aluminum foil.
6. **Rest the Chicken:**
    - Remove the chicken from the oven and let it rest for about 10-15 minutes before carving. This helps the juices redistribute and keeps the meat moist.
7. **Serve:**
    - Carve the chicken and serve with your favorite sides. You can also use the pan drippings to make a simple gravy if desired.

This Herb-Crusted Roasted Chicken has a fragrant, flavorful crust and juicy, tender meat, making it a perfect centerpiece for a meal. Enjoy!

Pacific Northwest Pumpkin Soup

Ingredients:

- 2 tablespoons olive oil or unsalted butter
- 1 large onion, diced
- 2 cloves garlic, minced
- 2 medium carrots, peeled and diced
- 2 celery stalks, diced
- 1 teaspoon ground cumin
- 1 teaspoon ground cinnamon
- 1/2 teaspoon ground nutmeg
- 4 cups pumpkin puree (fresh or canned)
- 4 cups vegetable broth (or chicken broth)
- 1 cup coconut milk or heavy cream
- 2 tablespoons maple syrup or honey (optional, for sweetness)
- Salt and freshly ground black pepper to taste
- 1/4 cup fresh parsley or cilantro, chopped (optional, for garnish)
- Pumpkin seeds or croutons (optional, for garnish)

Instructions:

1. **Sauté Vegetables:**
   - In a large pot or Dutch oven, heat the olive oil or butter over medium heat.
   - Add the diced onion, carrots, and celery. Sauté until the vegetables are softened, about 5-7 minutes.
   - Add the minced garlic and cook for another minute until fragrant.
2. **Add Spices:**
   - Stir in the ground cumin, cinnamon, and nutmeg. Cook for 1-2 minutes to toast the spices and enhance their flavors.
3. **Add Pumpkin and Broth:**
   - Add the pumpkin puree to the pot, stirring to combine with the vegetables and spices.
   - Pour in the vegetable broth and bring the mixture to a boil.
   - Reduce the heat to low and simmer for about 15-20 minutes to allow the flavors to meld.
4. **Blend the Soup:**
   - Use an immersion blender to puree the soup directly in the pot until smooth. Alternatively, you can carefully transfer the soup in batches to a countertop blender and blend until smooth.
5. **Finish the Soup:**
   - Return the blended soup to the pot (if using a countertop blender).
   - Stir in the coconut milk or heavy cream and maple syrup or honey (if using). Heat gently until warmed through.
   - Season with salt and freshly ground black pepper to taste.

6. **Serve:**
    - Ladle the soup into bowls.
    - Garnish with chopped fresh parsley or cilantro, and optionally, sprinkle with pumpkin seeds or croutons.

This Pacific Northwest Pumpkin Soup is creamy, spiced, and perfect for a cozy meal. Enjoy the rich flavors and comforting texture!

Apple-Walnut Pancakes

Ingredients:

- **For the Pancake Batter:**
    - 1 1/2 cups all-purpose flour
    - 2 tablespoons granulated sugar
    - 1 tablespoon baking powder
    - 1/2 teaspoon salt
    - 1 cup milk (any kind, including non-dairy)
    - 1 large egg
    - 2 tablespoons unsalted butter, melted (or oil for a dairy-free option)
    - 1 teaspoon vanilla extract
- **For the Apple-Walnut Filling:**
    - 1 large apple, peeled, cored, and diced
    - 1 tablespoon unsalted butter
    - 1 tablespoon granulated sugar
    - 1/2 teaspoon ground cinnamon
    - 1/2 cup walnuts, chopped and toasted
- **For Serving:**
    - Maple syrup or honey
    - Additional walnuts (optional)
    - Powdered sugar (optional)

Instructions:

1. **Prepare the Apple-Walnut Filling:**
    - In a skillet, melt 1 tablespoon of butter over medium heat.
    - Add the diced apple, sugar, and cinnamon. Cook, stirring occasionally, until the apples are tender and caramelized, about 5-7 minutes.
    - Stir in the chopped walnuts and cook for an additional 1-2 minutes. Remove from heat and set aside.
2. **Prepare the Pancake Batter:**
    - In a large bowl, whisk together the flour, sugar, baking powder, and salt.
    - In another bowl, combine the milk, egg, melted butter, and vanilla extract.
    - Pour the wet ingredients into the dry ingredients and stir until just combined. The batter may be a bit lumpy, which is fine.
3. **Cook the Pancakes:**
    - Heat a non-stick skillet or griddle over medium heat and lightly grease with butter or oil.
    - Pour 1/4 cup of batter onto the skillet for each pancake.
    - Cook until bubbles form on the surface of the pancake and the edges look set, about 2-3 minutes.
    - Flip the pancake and cook for an additional 1-2 minutes, or until golden brown and cooked through.

4. **Serve:**
    - Stack the pancakes on plates and top with the apple-walnut mixture.
    - Drizzle with maple syrup or honey.
    - Optionally, sprinkle with additional walnuts and powdered sugar.

These Apple-Walnut Pancakes are a wonderful combination of flavors and textures, making for a delicious and satisfying breakfast. Enjoy!

Spicy Salmon Sushi Rolls

Ingredients:

- **For the Sushi Rolls:**
    - 2 cups sushi rice (short-grain rice)
    - 2 1/2 cups water
    - 1/2 cup rice vinegar
    - 1/4 cup sugar
    - 1 teaspoon salt
    - 4 sheets nori (seaweed)
    - 1/2 pound fresh sushi-grade salmon, cut into thin strips
    - 1 avocado, sliced
    - 1 small cucumber, julienned
    - 1-2 tablespoons spicy mayo (see recipe below)
    - Soy sauce, for serving
    - Pickled ginger, for serving
    - Wasabi, for serving
- **For the Spicy Mayo:**
    - 1/4 cup mayonnaise
    - 1 tablespoon Sriracha (adjust to taste)
    - 1 teaspoon soy sauce
    - 1 teaspoon lemon juice

Instructions:

1. **Prepare the Sushi Rice:**
    - Rinse the sushi rice under cold water until the water runs clear. This removes excess starch.
    - Combine the rinsed rice and water in a rice cooker and cook according to the manufacturer's instructions. Alternatively, cook on the stovetop by bringing to a boil, then reducing heat to low, covering, and simmering for about 20 minutes.
2. **Season the Rice:**
    - While the rice is cooking, prepare the sushi vinegar. In a small saucepan, combine rice vinegar, sugar, and salt. Heat over low heat, stirring until the sugar and salt are dissolved. Do not boil.
    - Once the rice is cooked, transfer it to a large bowl and gently fold in the seasoned vinegar. Allow the rice to cool to room temperature before using.
3. **Prepare the Spicy Mayo:**
    - In a small bowl, mix together the mayonnaise, Sriracha, soy sauce, and lemon juice until well combined. Adjust the heat level to your preference.
4. **Assemble the Sushi Rolls:**
    - Place a bamboo sushi mat on a flat surface and lay a sheet of nori, shiny side down, on the mat.

- Wet your hands with water to prevent sticking and spread an even layer of sushi rice over the nori, leaving a 1-inch border at the top edge.
- Gently press the rice down with your fingers or the back of a spoon to ensure it sticks to the nori.
- Arrange strips of salmon, avocado slices, and cucumber julienne horizontally across the rice, about 1/3 of the way up from the bottom edge.
- Drizzle a little spicy mayo over the fillings.

5. **Roll the Sushi:**
   - Carefully lift the bamboo mat and start rolling the sushi from the bottom edge, pressing gently to keep the roll tight. Roll until you reach the exposed edge of the nori.
   - Seal the roll by moistening the edge of the nori with a little water and pressing to stick.
6. **Slice the Rolls:**
   - Use a sharp knife to slice the roll into 6-8 pieces. Clean the knife between cuts to ensure clean slices.
7. **Serve:**
   - Arrange the sushi rolls on a plate and serve with soy sauce, pickled ginger, and wasabi on the side.

These Spicy Salmon Sushi Rolls are flavorful, fresh, and have a delightful kick from the spicy mayo. Enjoy your homemade sushi!

Clam and Corn Bake

Ingredients:

- 4 cups fresh or frozen corn kernels (about 4-5 ears of corn, or 1 pound frozen)
- 2 cups canned or fresh clams, drained (reserve the clam juice if using canned)
- 1 cup milk
- 1/2 cup heavy cream
- 1/4 cup clam juice (optional, if not using canned clams)
- 2 tablespoons unsalted butter
- 1 small onion, finely chopped
- 2 cloves garlic, minced
- 1/2 teaspoon dried thyme
- 1/2 teaspoon dried oregano
- Salt and freshly ground black pepper to taste
- 1/2 cup grated Parmesan cheese
- 1/2 cup breadcrumbs (preferably panko for extra crunch)
- 2 tablespoons fresh parsley, chopped (optional, for garnish)

Instructions:

1. **Preheat Oven:**
   - Preheat your oven to 375°F (190°C).
2. **Prepare the Corn:**
   - If using fresh corn, remove the kernels from the cob. If using frozen corn, thaw it before use.
3. **Sauté Vegetables:**
   - In a large skillet, melt the butter over medium heat.
   - Add the chopped onion and cook until softened and translucent, about 5 minutes.
   - Add the minced garlic and cook for another minute until fragrant.
4. **Combine Ingredients:**
   - Stir in the corn and cook for another 2-3 minutes.
   - Add the clams, milk, heavy cream, clam juice (if using), dried thyme, and dried oregano. Stir to combine.
   - Season with salt and freshly ground black pepper to taste.
   - Cook for an additional 5 minutes, allowing the mixture to heat through and flavors to meld.
5. **Prepare the Topping:**
   - In a small bowl, mix together the grated Parmesan cheese and breadcrumbs.
6. **Assemble the Bake:**
   - Transfer the corn and clam mixture to a baking dish (about 9x9 inches or similar size).
   - Sprinkle the Parmesan and breadcrumb mixture evenly over the top.
7. **Bake:**

- Bake in the preheated oven for 20-25 minutes, or until the topping is golden brown and the mixture is bubbly.

8. **Garnish and Serve:**
    - Remove from the oven and let it cool slightly before serving.
    - Garnish with fresh parsley if desired.

This Clam and Corn Bake is creamy, savory, and has a delightful crunch from the breadcrumb topping. It's a fantastic way to enjoy the flavors of the sea combined with the sweetness of corn. Enjoy!

Cherry-Almond Coffee Cake

Ingredients:

- **For the Cake:**
    - 1 1/2 cups all-purpose flour
    - 1 cup granulated sugar
    - 1/2 cup unsalted butter, softened
    - 1/2 cup sour cream or Greek yogurt
    - 2 large eggs
    - 1 teaspoon vanilla extract
    - 1 teaspoon baking powder
    - 1/2 teaspoon baking soda
    - 1/4 teaspoon salt
    - 1 cup fresh or frozen cherries, pitted and halved (if using frozen, do not thaw)
- **For the Almond Topping:**
    - 1/4 cup sliced almonds
    - 2 tablespoons granulated sugar
    - 1/2 teaspoon ground cinnamon
- **For the Glaze (optional):**
    - 1/2 cup powdered sugar
    - 1-2 tablespoons milk or cream
    - 1/4 teaspoon almond extract (optional)

Instructions:

1. **Preheat Oven:**
    - Preheat your oven to 350°F (175°C). Grease and flour a 9-inch round cake pan or line it with parchment paper.
2. **Prepare the Cake Batter:**
    - In a medium bowl, whisk together the flour, baking powder, baking soda, and salt.
    - In a large bowl, cream the softened butter and granulated sugar together until light and fluffy.
    - Beat in the eggs one at a time, then add the vanilla extract and mix well.
    - Gradually add the flour mixture to the butter mixture, alternating with the sour cream or Greek yogurt. Begin and end with the flour mixture, mixing until just combined.
    - Gently fold in the cherries.
3. **Prepare the Almond Topping:**
    - In a small bowl, combine the sliced almonds, granulated sugar, and ground cinnamon.
4. **Assemble the Cake:**
    - Pour the cake batter into the prepared cake pan and smooth the top with a spatula.
    - Sprinkle the almond topping evenly over the batter.

5. **Bake:**
   - Bake in the preheated oven for 35-45 minutes, or until a toothpick inserted into the center of the cake comes out clean and the top is golden brown.
6. **Cool and Glaze:**
   - Allow the cake to cool in the pan for about 10 minutes, then transfer to a wire rack to cool completely.
   - If desired, prepare the glaze by mixing the powdered sugar with milk or cream until smooth. Add almond extract if using. Drizzle over the cooled cake.
7. **Serve:**
   - Slice and serve the Cherry-Almond Coffee Cake as a delightful treat with coffee or tea.

This Cherry-Almond Coffee Cake is rich, flavorful, and has a wonderful blend of tart cherries and nutty almonds. Enjoy!

Grilled Portobello Mushrooms

Ingredients:

- 4 large portobello mushrooms, stems removed and gills scraped out
- 1/4 cup olive oil
- 2 tablespoons balsamic vinegar
- 2 cloves garlic, minced
- 1 tablespoon fresh rosemary, chopped (or 1 teaspoon dried rosemary)
- 1 teaspoon fresh thyme leaves (or 1/2 teaspoon dried thyme)
- 1 teaspoon Dijon mustard
- Salt and freshly ground black pepper to taste
- Optional: 1/4 teaspoon red pepper flakes (for a bit of heat)

Instructions:

1. **Prepare the Marinade:**
   - In a small bowl, whisk together the olive oil, balsamic vinegar, minced garlic, chopped rosemary, thyme, Dijon mustard, salt, black pepper, and red pepper flakes if using.
2. **Marinate the Mushrooms:**
   - Place the portobello mushrooms in a large resealable plastic bag or shallow dish.
   - Pour the marinade over the mushrooms, making sure they are well-coated. If using a bag, seal it and gently toss to coat. If using a dish, turn the mushrooms a few times to ensure even coverage.
   - Let the mushrooms marinate in the refrigerator for at least 30 minutes, or up to 2 hours for a deeper flavor.
3. **Preheat the Grill:**
   - Preheat your grill to medium-high heat (about 375°F to 400°F or 190°C to 200°C). If using a gas grill, oil the grates or use a grill brush to clean them.
4. **Grill the Mushrooms:**
   - Remove the mushrooms from the marinade and let any excess drip off.
   - Place the mushrooms gill-side down on the grill.
   - Grill for about 4-5 minutes on each side, or until they are tender and have nice grill marks. The mushrooms should be cooked through and have a juicy interior.
5. **Serve:**
   - Remove the mushrooms from the grill and let them rest for a few minutes.
   - Serve the grilled portobello mushrooms as a main dish or a side. They are great on their own or sliced and added to salads, sandwiches, or burgers.

Optional:

- You can top the grilled mushrooms with a sprinkle of feta cheese or fresh herbs for added flavor.
- Serve with a squeeze of fresh lemon juice for a bright finish.

These Grilled Portobello Mushrooms are savory and satisfying, making them a great vegetarian option for your grilling repertoire. Enjoy!

Washington State Fruit Tart

Ingredients:

- **For the Tart Crust:**
    - 1 1/2 cups all-purpose flour
    - 1/4 cup granulated sugar
    - 1/2 teaspoon salt
    - 1/2 cup unsalted butter, cold and cut into small pieces
    - 1 large egg yolk
    - 2-3 tablespoons ice water
- **For the Cream Filling:**
    - 1 cup heavy cream
    - 1/2 cup mascarpone cheese
    - 1/4 cup powdered sugar
    - 1 teaspoon vanilla extract
- **For the Fruit Topping:**
    - 1 cup fresh berries (such as blueberries, raspberries, or blackberries)
    - 1-2 apples or pears, thinly sliced
    - 1-2 peaches or plums, thinly sliced
    - Optional: a handful of fresh mint leaves for garnish
- **For the Glaze (optional):**
    - 1/4 cup apricot or peach jam
    - 1 tablespoon water

Instructions:

1. **Prepare the Tart Crust:**
    - In a medium bowl, whisk together the flour, sugar, and salt.
    - Cut in the cold butter using a pastry cutter or your fingers until the mixture resembles coarse crumbs.
    - Add the egg yolk and mix until combined.
    - Gradually add ice water, one tablespoon at a time, until the dough comes together. It should be moist but not sticky.
    - Shape the dough into a disk, wrap in plastic wrap, and refrigerate for at least 30 minutes.
2. **Preheat Oven:**
    - Preheat your oven to 375°F (190°C).
3. **Roll Out and Bake the Crust:**
    - On a lightly floured surface, roll out the dough to fit a 9-inch tart pan. Transfer the dough to the pan, pressing it into the edges and trimming any excess.
    - Prick the bottom of the crust with a fork to prevent bubbling.
    - Bake for 15-20 minutes, or until the crust is golden brown. Let it cool completely on a wire rack.
4. **Prepare the Cream Filling:**

- In a medium bowl, whip the heavy cream until stiff peaks form.
- Gently fold in the mascarpone cheese, powdered sugar, and vanilla extract until smooth and well combined.

5. **Assemble the Tart:**
    - Spread the cream filling evenly over the cooled tart crust.
    - Arrange the fresh fruit on top of the cream filling in a decorative pattern.
6. **Prepare the Glaze (optional):**
    - In a small saucepan, heat the apricot or peach jam with water until melted and smooth.
    - Brush the glaze over the fruit to give it a shiny finish and help preserve freshness.
7. **Garnish and Serve:**
    - Garnish with fresh mint leaves if desired.
    - Chill the tart in the refrigerator until ready to serve.

This Washington State Fruit Tart is a delightful way to enjoy fresh, seasonal fruits with a creamy filling and buttery crust. It's perfect for a special occasion or a refreshing summer dessert. Enjoy!

Spaghetti with Tomato and Basil

Ingredients:

- 12 ounces (340 grams) spaghetti
- 2 tablespoons olive oil
- 4 cloves garlic, minced
- 1 can (14.5 ounces) diced tomatoes (or 4-5 cups fresh tomatoes, peeled and chopped)
- 1/4 cup tomato paste
- 1 teaspoon dried oregano
- 1/2 teaspoon red pepper flakes (optional, for a bit of heat)
- Salt and freshly ground black pepper to taste
- 1/4 cup fresh basil leaves, chopped
- 1/4 cup grated Parmesan cheese (optional, for serving)
- Fresh basil leaves for garnish (optional)

Instructions:

1. **Cook the Spaghetti:**
   - Bring a large pot of salted water to a boil.
   - Add the spaghetti and cook according to the package instructions until al dente.
   - Reserve 1/2 cup of pasta water, then drain the spaghetti and set aside.
2. **Prepare the Tomato Sauce:**
   - While the pasta is cooking, heat the olive oil in a large skillet over medium heat.
   - Add the minced garlic and sauté for about 1 minute, until fragrant but not browned.
   - Stir in the diced tomatoes and tomato paste, and cook for about 5 minutes, allowing the sauce to simmer and thicken slightly.
   - Add the dried oregano, red pepper flakes (if using), salt, and pepper. Adjust the seasoning to taste.
   - Stir in the chopped basil and cook for another 1-2 minutes, until the basil is wilted and the sauce is well combined.
3. **Combine Pasta and Sauce:**
   - Add the cooked spaghetti to the skillet with the tomato sauce.
   - Toss the pasta and sauce together, adding a bit of the reserved pasta water if needed to help the sauce coat the pasta evenly.
4. **Serve:**
   - Divide the spaghetti among serving plates.
   - Sprinkle with grated Parmesan cheese if desired.
   - Garnish with additional fresh basil leaves.

This Spaghetti with Tomato and Basil is a timeless favorite that's both easy to make and packed with fresh flavors. Enjoy your meal!

Crab-Stuffed Mushrooms

Ingredients:

- 12 large cremini or button mushrooms
- 2 tablespoons olive oil
- 1 small onion, finely chopped
- 2 cloves garlic, minced
- 1 cup fresh crab meat (lump or claw meat, preferably)
- 1/2 cup cream cheese, softened
- 1/4 cup mayonnaise
- 1/4 cup grated Parmesan cheese
- 1 tablespoon fresh parsley, chopped (plus extra for garnish)
- 1 teaspoon lemon juice
- 1/2 teaspoon dried thyme
- Salt and freshly ground black pepper to taste
- 1/2 cup panko breadcrumbs

Instructions:

1. **Preheat Oven:**
    - Preheat your oven to 375°F (190°C).
2. **Prepare the Mushrooms:**
    - Clean the mushrooms with a damp cloth.
    - Gently remove the stems and set the caps aside. Finely chop the mushroom stems.
3. **Cook the Filling:**
    - Heat the olive oil in a skillet over medium heat.
    - Add the chopped mushroom stems, onion, and garlic. Sauté until the mixture is softened and the onions are translucent, about 5 minutes.
    - Remove from heat and let cool slightly.
4. **Prepare the Crab Mixture:**
    - In a medium bowl, combine the cream cheese, mayonnaise, grated Parmesan cheese, chopped parsley, lemon juice, dried thyme, salt, and pepper.
    - Fold in the cooked mushroom stem mixture and the crab meat. Mix gently until well combined.
5. **Stuff the Mushrooms:**
    - Place the mushroom caps on a baking sheet lined with parchment paper or a lightly greased baking dish.
    - Spoon the crab mixture into each mushroom cap, pressing down slightly to pack the filling.
6. **Prepare the Topping:**
    - In a small bowl, mix the panko breadcrumbs with a little olive oil or melted butter. Sprinkle the breadcrumb mixture evenly over the stuffed mushrooms.
7. **Bake:**

- Bake in the preheated oven for 15-20 minutes, or until the mushrooms are tender and the topping is golden brown.
8. **Garnish and Serve:**
    - Remove from the oven and let cool slightly.
    - Garnish with additional chopped parsley if desired.

These Crab-Stuffed Mushrooms are flavorful, rich, and perfect for a special occasion or a tasty appetizer. Enjoy!

Marionberry and Cream Cheese Bars

Ingredients:

- **For the Crust:**
    - 1 1/2 cups all-purpose flour
    - 1/2 cup granulated sugar
    - 1/2 teaspoon baking powder
    - 1/4 teaspoon salt
    - 1/2 cup unsalted butter, cold and cut into small pieces
- **For the Cream Cheese Layer:**
    - 8 ounces cream cheese, softened
    - 1/2 cup granulated sugar
    - 1 large egg
    - 1 teaspoon vanilla extract
- **For the Marionberry Filling:**
    - 2 cups fresh or frozen marionberries (if using frozen, thaw and drain them)
    - 1/2 cup granulated sugar
    - 2 tablespoons cornstarch
    - 1 tablespoon lemon juice

Instructions:

1. **Preheat Oven:**
    - Preheat your oven to 350°F (175°C). Grease a 9x9-inch baking dish or line it with parchment paper.
2. **Prepare the Crust:**
    - In a medium bowl, combine the flour, sugar, baking powder, and salt.
    - Cut in the cold butter using a pastry cutter or your fingers until the mixture resembles coarse crumbs.
    - Press the mixture into the bottom of the prepared baking dish to form an even layer.
    - Bake for 10-12 minutes, or until lightly golden. Remove from the oven and set aside.
3. **Prepare the Marionberry Filling:**
    - In a medium saucepan, combine the marionberries, sugar, cornstarch, and lemon juice.
    - Cook over medium heat, stirring frequently, until the mixture comes to a boil and thickens, about 5-7 minutes.
    - Remove from heat and let cool slightly.
4. **Prepare the Cream Cheese Layer:**
    - In a medium bowl, beat the softened cream cheese with an electric mixer until smooth.
    - Add the sugar, egg, and vanilla extract, and beat until well combined.
5. **Assemble the Bars:**

        - Spread the cream cheese mixture evenly over the pre-baked crust.
        - Spoon the marionberry filling over the cream cheese layer, spreading it out gently with the back of a spoon or a spatula.
6. **Bake:**
        - Bake in the preheated oven for 25-30 minutes, or until the cream cheese layer is set and the edges are lightly browned.
        - Let the bars cool completely in the pan on a wire rack before cutting into squares.
7. **Serve:**
        - Cut into squares and serve. These bars are delicious on their own or with a dusting of powdered sugar.

These Marionberry and Cream Cheese Bars offer a delightful combination of tangy berries and creamy filling, all atop a buttery crust. Enjoy!